Holiday Sweets Without Sugar

Books by Michael and Nina Shandler

The Marriage and Family Book
Yoga for Pregnancy and Birth
Ways of Being Together
How to Make All the "Meat" You Eat from Wheat
Homemade Mixes for Instant Meals the Natural Way
The Complete Guide and Cookbook for Raising
Your Child as a Vegetarian

RAWSON, WADE PUBLISHERS, INC. New York

Holiday Sweets Without Sugar

NINA AND MICHAEL SHANDLER

Library of Congress Cataloging in Publication Data
Shandler, Nina.
Holiday sweets without sugar.

Includes index.
1. Desserts.   2. Confectionery.   3. Sugar-free diet—
Recipes.   I. Shandler, Michael.   II. Title.
TX773.S427   641.8′6   81-40274
ISBN 0-89256-188-2   AACR2
ISBN 0-89256-189-0 (pbk.)

Published simultaneously in Canada by McClelland and Stewart, Ltd.
Composition by American–Stratford Graphic Services, Inc.,
Brattleboro, Vermont
Printed and bound by R. R. Donnelley & Sons Co., Crawfordsville, Indiana

Designed by Jacques Chazaud

First Edition

With much love
to Nina's parents, Mabel and Carl Silverberg, who pa-
tiently endured her cooking experimentation and the
resulting devastation of their kitchen throughout her
childhood.

Contents

CHAPTER ONE: Unique Techniques for Creating Naturally Sweet Treats   *3*

    Desserts for the Calorie Conscious   *5*

    Treats for the Diabetic   *6*

    Sweets for Hypoglycemics   *7*

    Holiday Snacks for Children   *8*

    Unique Techniques for Light Desserts from Whole Grains   *8*

    Foods for Creating Naturally Sweet Treats   *10*

CHAPTER TWO: Repeatedly Used Recipes   *15*

CHAPTER THREE: Christmas—Hanukkah: A Holiday Season of Healthy Treats   *21*

    Children's Christmas or Hanukkah Treats   *47*

CHAPTER FOUR: Natural Treats for the New Year   *51*

CHAPTER FIVE: Healthy Hearts, Candies and Cakes for Valentine's Day   *65*
    Children's Valentine's Treats   *84*

CHAPTER SIX: Heavenly Easter Goodies   *87*
    Children's Easter Treats   *110*

CHAPTER SEVEN: Midsummer Fresh Fruit Desserts for the Fourth of July   *113*
    Children's July Fourth Treats   *136*

CHAPTER EIGHT: Fall Fun Foods for Halloween   *141*
    Children's Trick-O'-Treats   *158*

CHAPTER NINE: A Thanksgiving Harvest of Naturally Sweet Desserts   *161*

INDEX   *183*

Holiday Sweets Without Sugar

1

Unique Techniques for Creating Naturally Sweet Treats

Every holiday has its casualties: natural foods diets forsaken, painfully shed pounds regained, children's teeth assaulted, hypoglycemics and diabetics deprived. The major cause of these unwelcome side effects is sugar. Its sweet seductive taste tempts us to overeat enormous quantities of high-calorie, nutritionally deficient "goodies" at Thanksgiving, Christmas, Hanukkah, Valentine's Day, and on all those other special occasions.

At these celebrations, those of us who have resolved to cut down on or eliminate sugar from our diets need alternatives that are just as appealing as candy canes and chocolates. Cakes that look and taste like heavy whole wheat bread offer little consolation. Cookies with the feel of Rye Krisp crackers don't eliminate temptation. Desserts made with honey don't reduce calories or tooth decay.

To resolve the holiday sugar blues, light, moist cakes, airy parfaits, delicate breads and fancy pastries made without refined white sugar, brown sugar, table molasses, corn syrup, honey or maple syrup, are the optimum prescription. If these tempting naturally sweet treats can be made with whole grains, they become a nutritionally positive part of our daily fare as well, since they add a large spectrum of vitamins, minerals and amino acids to each delicious mouthful. With such sweet foods available, eating "health" food or minimizing both calories and carbohydrates is no sacrifice—even on celebration days.

The recipes in this book fit that description. They are made with naturally sweet foods—no empty calories; they use only whole grains—no artificially enriched flours. Best of all, they will satisfy the urge for something especially fancy, light and tasty to eat at parties, to give as holiday presents or feed celebrating children. There are simple little tricks in these pages for making foods sweet and grains light. Fruit juices and frozen juice concentrates, especially apple juice and apple concentrate, are most commonly used. Other naturally sweet ingredients include fresh fruits, dried fruits, carob powder, non-instant dried milk powder, and unsweetened shredded coconut. (See pages 10–13 for a lengthier description of these and other ingredients, as well as recommendations about where to buy them.)

In many of the recipes, blackstrap molasses or malt are called upon for a specific taste or texture. These concentrated sweetners, unlike refined sugar products, honey, or even maple syrup, are rich in nutrients. Malt, which is made by slowly cooking sprouted barley, contains B-complex vitamins, the amino acid lysine, and many essential minerals. Blackstrap molasses, which is the residue of the sugar cane after the sugar is extracted, contains more iron per unit of weight than eggs, more calcium than milk, more potassium than any other food, and is rich in several other minerals and vitamins. Because of its extraordinary food value, it is often recommended as a supplemental food by nutritionists and nutritionally aware doctors.

The taste of the naturally sweet treats in this cookbook is greatly enhanced by the use of spices and natural flavorings such as cinnamon, cardamom, allspice, ginger, nutmeg, orange peel, lemon peel, vanilla extract, almond extract and peppermint extract. By relying on the natural sweetness of foods and pure flavorings, it is not difficult to make desserts that are substantially lower both in calories and in carbohydrates than their conventional counterparts.

Desserts for the Calorie Conscious

The weight-conscious person will be delighted by these naturally sweet desserts. She or he can enjoy holidays without worrying about gaining extra pounds, and will be able to serve and indulge in these low-calorie treats many other times during the year. Apple juice and apple juice concentrate are often the only sweetening and liquid used in a cake, cookie, or dessert bread recipe. Typically, a cup of juice is only 80 calories and 2 tablespoons of concentrate are a mere 48 calories.

Thus, all of the sweetening and liquid necessary for a recipe that serves 6 to 8 people adds up to a mere 128 calories. In contrast, *the sugar and milk in a conventional recipe would add up to 950 calories.* So this simple method of baking has already saved you *over 800 calories in just one recipe.* And for those accustomed to using honey, the savings may be even greater since a cup of honey contains 1,031 calories!

To cut calories even further, confectioners' sugar may be replaced by non-instant skim milk powder in frosting; roasted carob powder can be used instead of cocoa; and skim milk ricotta cheese, blended with apple juice concentrate, is a good substitute for whipped cream or cream cheese. These and other simple, healthful, weight-saving tricks can be found in virtually every recipe in this cookbook.

All of our recipes are lower in calories than conventional recipes, *and many are extremely low.* To aid those who want to count calories, we have made a rough estimate of the calorie content of these recipes, identifying each as "under 150 calories per serving," "approximately 150 calories per serving," "approximately 225 calories per serving," or "over 250 calories per serving."

Treats for the Diabetic

Diabetics must be particularly careful to consume carbohydrates, proteins and fats in proper amounts and proportions, according to the directions of their physicians. Since diabetics with severe cases must adhere to these guidelines rigidly, each recipe in this or any cookbook should be analyzed to determine its appropriateness for the individual. Those with less severe cases, however, will benefit greatly from this cookbook since the most concentrated carbohydrate—sugar—is entirely eliminated.

Carbohydrate-conscious cooks will note that we have included rough estimates of the carbohydrate content of our recipes. Low-carbohydrate recipes are designated as containing approximately 20 grams or less of carbohydrates. Moderate carbohydrate recipes are identified as containing roughly 30 grams per serving, and recipes that are higher in carbohydrates are identified as over 35 grams per serving. If you are using the conventional exchange system for diabetics, our low-carbohydrate recipes are roughly equivalent to one fruit exchange.

It should also be noted that the generally accepted dietary recommendations for diabetics have become the subject of some controversy. Researchers are now experimenting with fruits and high-fiber foods to determine whether they might prove beneficial to diabetics. Paavo Airola, the noted nutritionist, reports in *How to Get Well* that fructose does not require insulin for assimilation, and therefore may be an appropriate sweetener for diabetics. According to the editors of *Prevention* magazine, research indicates that whole grains and other high-fiber foods, notably chestnuts and yams, are being used with success on an experimental group of diabetics.

Such research may pave the way for diabetics to enjoy the vast majority of the recipes in this book in the future. However, since these results are not yet conclusive, any deviation from a prescribed diabetic diet should be discussed with a knowledgeable physician or nutritionist.

Sweets for Hypoglycemics

Perhaps the disease that generates the most dietary controversy is hypoglycemia, or low blood sugar. Traditionally, a high-protein, low-carbohydrate diet was prescribed. However, an increasing number of nutritionists and nutritionally aware doctors are now recommending a diet moderate in protein and high in *unrefined* carbohydrates. Since the hypoglycemic needs to keep his or her blood sugar level constant, with no sudden increases or decreases, whole grains that burn slowly and steadily are thought to be extremely beneficial. Small amounts of fruit and fruit juices can also be safely tolerated by hypoglycemics since these substances regulate blood sugar effectively. The hypoglycemic following this high unrefined carbohydrate diet will be able to use the majority of our recipes. However, severe hypoglycemia, like diabetes, is a serious disease, and sufferers should taken care not to overindulge in sweets, even naturally sweet treats.

Holiday Snacks for Children

Children whose parents place limits on their sugar and/or white flour intake, will greet the holiday treats designed especially for them with great enthusiasm. They can enjoy Santa Claus cookies, Valentine's Day candies, Easter bunny goodies and Halloween treats without parental lectures or warnings.

Unique Techniques for Light Desserts from Whole Grains

Since whole grain flours are high in fiber and have a wider range of nutrients than enriched refined wheat flour, we have experimented extensively with them to achieve a lightness that normally is missing from "health food" sweets, cakes, yeasted breads and pastries. To successfully bake desserts using whole grains takes more personal judgment and experience than baking with white flour. Whole grain flours vary in the amount of liquids they absorb depending on two factors: the hardness of the particular crop and the texture of the grind. These uncontrollable variables have implications for all your baking.

Cakes

It should be remembered that whole-grain cake batters, like white flour batters, need to be quite liquid. If the batter is too dense the cake will be heavy. Occasionally, it may be necessary to use slightly less flour mixture than called for in the recipe. Therefore, add the flour mixture gradually to the liquids, stopping when the proper texture is achieved. If the consistency is right and the flours are well mixed, your cake will be nearly as light as a white flour cake.

To achieve a light texture, *a combination of whole grain flours is best.* Whole wheat pastry flour holds moisture and brown rice flour creates airiness.

Eggs, especially when whites are beaten separately and folded into batters, provide extra lightness.

Whole Grain Dessert Breads

Yeasted dessert breads from whole grains can be given the texture and feel of white flour sweet breads *by adding gluten flour and soy flour to whole wheat pastry flour.* The resulting doughnuts, coffee cakes and sweet rolls are not only light and delicious but also extremely high in complete protein. They often pack as much as 10 grams of protein in a single serving!

By combining pastry flour with gluten flour, you can create cream puff pastry equal to the delicacy of white flour cream puffs. The resulting puffs can be filled with a vast number of festive, healthful, low-calorie custards and cremes.

Cream Puff Pastry

Surprisingly light and flaky pie crusts can be made totally without white flour. By combining whole wheat pastry flour, gluten flour and soy flour, to make a slightly damp pastry dough, pastries that are both delicate and extremely high in protein and other nutrients can decorate your holiday table as well as your daily dinner table.

Pie Crusts

Whole wheat pastry flour makes a wonderful strudel. Combined with egg and vinegar, it can be stretched to a paper-thin consistency for the delicate texture so enjoyable in an old-fashioned strudel.

Strudel

Creating, testing and tasting *Holiday Sweets Without Sugar* has been a joy for our whole family, which includes two sweet-loving children, one hypoglycemic and a reformed sugar addict. Even Grandma and Grandpa have reaped unexpected benefits. It's been our custom for the last two or three years to spend extended teatimes with grandparents, once or twice a month. These pleasant Saturday afternoons always involved two markedly different menus. There was our whole grain bread, or crackers, and cheese and some admittedly heavy health food cake. Then, there was Grandma's homebaked coffee bread, cake or chocolate chip cookies. The children would, of course, look at us with pleading eyes and ask, "Can I have just one of Grandma's?" We would hesitantly answer "Just one!" As the afternoon progressed, even we sugar-conscious adults would find ourselves self-consciously fingering our way toward the coffee cake and taking "just a little sliver," and then another and another. This ritual changed quite dramatically when the experiments for this book began working.

Grandma and Grandpa began eying our carob cakes, éclairs and apple pies. They began taking "just a little bit" of our dessert fare and even the children began foregoing Grandma's superb sugar goodies. The transition to naturally sweet treats for Grandma and Grandpa's visits was voted a complete success when Grandma, quite without prompting, suggested that I make the birthday cake for Michael and Grandpa, whose birthdays fall just two days apart. We had a Carob Strawberry Cheese Roll that everyone shared with equal pleasure.

Foods for Creating Naturally Sweet Treats

Frozen apple juice concentrate is an unsweetened juice concentrate that can be found in large supermarkets in the frozen juice section. Thawed and used directly in these recipes, it provides greater sweetness than apple juice or cider.

Frozen pineapple juice concentrate can be found in the freezer section of most large grocery stores. It adds the sweetness and flavor of pineapple juice in a more concentrated form, and is useful when pineapple flavor is desired.

Unsweetened canned fruit packed in juice is available in almost every major brand of canned fruit. Peaches, pears, pineapple and, sometimes, cherries are easy to find in many supermarkets, and the cans are clearly marked "no sugar added."

Unsweetened frozen fruit can also be found in major supermarkets. Whole strawberries are the most readily available, but major brands also package black cherries, blueberries, melon balls and peaches without sugar.

Strawberry concentrate can be found in health and natural food stores. It is not frozen, but bottled. Hain is the most common major brand. Strawberry concentrate adds both sweetness and the special flavor of strawberries to recipes.

White grape juice has a particularly delicate sweet taste. It is available in a number of brands in all health and natural foods stores. It can often be found in supermarkets, too, since Welch's makes white grape juice as well as their popular purple grape juice.

Liquid barley malt is the same malt used for brewing beer. It is a thick syrup with a caramel flavor, and is available in most well-stocked natural foods stores. It can sometimes be found in supermarkets near the molasses. Be certain, however, not to buy malt that is hops-flavored. This type of malt is too bitter to be used for baking.

Blackstrap molasses can be bought in health and natural foods stores. It has a distinctive flavor, and in small amounts it can be used advantageously in many recipes. Blackstrap molasses should not be confused with table molasses which is lighter in color, less flavorful and high in sugar. Blackstrap is the residue of sugar cane after the sugar is removed, and it is highly nutritious.

Natural crème de menthe flavoring is a concentrated combination of mint flavor and alcohol. It is readily available in the spice section of major supermarkets.

Grain coffee substitute comes in many common brands including Pero, Bamboo, Caro and Cafix. These roasted grains are ground into a fine powder that can be mixed instantly into hot water or used in baking. These brands can be purchased at any health or natural foods store.

Burry's Health Food Carob Bars contain no sugar of any kind. These 3-ounce bars can be found in most health or natural foods stores and, when grated, make a wonderful sugar-free addition to many recipes.

Roasted carob powder is a dark flour made by milling carob pods and then roasting the flour. It is available at natural foods and health food stores. The powder gives recipes the flavor and sweetness of dark or bittersweet chocolate, but unlike chocolate, it is highly nutritious. Be sure to buy carob powder that has been roasted because the unroasted variety, although sweet, is not as rich or chocolate-like. It's easy to recognize the difference. The roasted powder is dark, similar in color to bittersweet chocolate bars. The unroasted powder has the lighter brown color of commercial cocoa drink mixes.

Brown rice flour is ground from whole grain brown rice, and adds lightness to cakes. It is readily available at health and natural foods stores. It should always be refrigerated because it will go rancid if left at room temperature for extended periods of time.

Gluten flour is the gluten extraction of wheat flour, and a small amount will add lightness to yeasted breads and pastry dough. The variety called for in these recipes is 80 percent gluten flour, which is extraordinarily high in protein—over 80 grams per cup. It is available in most health and natural foods stores. Be sure not to buy gluten flour bread mix, which is unbleached white flour that contains only a small amount of gluten flour. Although this type of flour is advertised as "high gluten," it will not have the same lightening effect.

Soy flour is created by grinding soybeans to a powder. It is available in health and natural foods stores. Soy flour loses its raw bean flavor in baked goods, and adds both lightness and protein.

Whole wheat pastry flour is ground from soft wheat. It is a finer powder than common whole wheat flour, and therefore is suitable for dessert baking. It is widely available at health and natural foods stores.

Unsalted butter is always recommended in this cookbook. It adds sweetness while providing oil content. It can be found in all well-stocked grocery stores.

Safflower oil is the oil we recommend in this cookbook. If you prefer to use another type, make sure it's cold-pressed. Generally, cold-pressed oils are only available in natural foods and health food stores. Sunflower oil can always be substituted for safflower oil in dessert baking. Both are light and delicate.

Baking powder without aluminum is available in health and natural foods stores. Rumford's baking powder is a commercial brand sometimes found in supermarkets that is also free of toxic aluminum.

Non-instant skim milk powder provides the nutrition and sweetness of milk in a more concentrated form. This fine powder is a versatile ingredient for creating sugarless treats. It is available at health and natural foods stores, and should not be confused with the granular milk powder found in supermarkets.

Granular lecithin is available at health and natural foods stores. It is commonly used as a food supplement, but when cooked it adds a smooth texture to desserts. It is often used in commercial candy bars to solidify chocolate.

Sesame tahini is a smooth seed butter resembling nut butters. It adds a delicate texture and a distinctive taste to many desserts. It is readily available in natural foods stores and gourmet shops.

2

Repeatedly Used Recipes

FLAKY PASTRY DOUGH   *(for Double Crust)*

1½ cups whole wheat pastry
   flour
¼ cup gluten flour
½ cup soy flour
⅓ cup safflower or sunflower oil
3 to 5 tablespoons ice water

In a bowl, combine pastry flour, gluten flour and soy flour with a wire whisk. With a fork, blend in oil to form a coarse meal. Stir in ice water 1 tablespoon at a time to form a moist pastry dough. Wrap in wax paper or plastic wrap and refrigerate for 30 minutes until chilled. Roll out between sheets of wax paper and bake according to recipe instructions.

STRETCHY PASTRY DOUGH   *(for Double Crust)*

1¼ cups whole wheat pastry
   flour
¼ cup gluten flour
½ cup soy flour
⅓ cup soft unsalted butter
6 to 8 tablespoons ice water

In a bowl, mix pastry flour, gluten flour and soy flour with a wire whisk. Rub butter into mixture with fingers to form a coarse meal. Stir in ice water 1 tablespoon at a time with a fork to form a ball of dough. Wrap in wax paper and chill for 30 minutes. Roll out on a board floured with cornstarch and bake according to recipe instructions.

CRUMBLE CRUST

(for 10-inch springform pan, including sides)

1 cup whole wheat pastry flour
½ cup rolled oats
½ cup raw wheat germ
⅓ cup unsweetened shredded
 coconut or chopped nuts (optional)
⅓ cup oil
2 tablespoons ice water or cold
 apple juice

Place flour, oats and wheat germ in an electric blender or food processor. Process until oatmeal resembles coarse meal. Place in a bowl and stir in coconut or chopped nuts (if desired). With a fork, stir in oil, then ice water or apple juice. Press into a springform pan and line sides. Bake or chill as recipe requires.

STRUDEL

(for 4 12-inch strudels)

¾ cup lukewarm water
1 egg, lightly beaten
¼ teaspoon vinegar
3 tablespoons melted butter
½ teaspoon salt
2½ cups whole wheat pastry
 flour
⅓ cup melted butter
1 cup fine whole wheat bread
 crumbs

In a bowl, beat together water, egg, vinegar and melted butter. In another bowl, combine salt and flour. Pour liquids into flour and beat with a wooden spoon for 5 minutes. Turn dough onto a floured board and knead for 10 minutes until smooth and elastic. If dough becomes sticky, knead in additional flour as necessary. Oil dough, cover and let stand 30 minutes. Prepare filling as desired.

Preheat oven to 450 degrees. Cover table with a clean cotton sheet or tablecloth. Sprinkle entire surface with flour. Roll dough to a paper-thin rectangle 4 x 6 feet. Brush whole surface with melted butter and sprinkle with bread crumbs. Spoon filling along 4-foot edge of pastry. Carefully lift tablecloth on the side where the filling has been placed. By lifting the cloth higher and higher, the entire strudel will roll over and over to form a delicate many-layered strudel. Cut into sections. Press sides of each section to form a seam.

Place on 2 well-oiled baking sheets. Brush with additional butter. Slash with a sharp knife every 2 inches across the top. Bake for 10 minutes. Reduce heat to 400 and bake for 20 minutes longer until golden and crisp.

DELICATE WHOLE WHEAT CRÊPES

(Makes 18 crêpes)

4 eggs
1 cup whole wheat pastry flour
½ cup milk
½ cup water
2 tablespoons melted butter

Combine all ingredients in a bowl. Beat with an electric mixer until batter resembles the consistency of light cream. Let stand for 2 hours before frying. Lightly oil a 6-inch heavy crêpe pan and heat over medium heat. Spoon 2½ tablespoons of batter in pan. Swirl pan to coat evenly with batter. Cook until crêpe easily shakes loose from pan. Turn and lightly brown second side. Use as directed in recipe.

LOW CALORIE EGGLESS CRÊPES

(Makes 18 crêpes)

⅔ cup corn flour
1⅓ cups whole wheat pastry flour
6 cups water
1 tablespoon oil
¼ tablespoon salt

Combine all ingredients in a bowl. Beat at high speed for 5 minutes with an electric mixer. Let stand for 2 hours and beat with a wire whisk just before cooking. Heat a lightly oiled 6-inch crêpe pan over medium-high heat. Pour ⅓ cup of crêpe batter into pan. Swirl to cover pan evenly and completely. Cook until edges of crêpe curl slightly or until crêpe can be freed easily from pan. Carefully turn to brown second side. Use as desired.

CREAM PUFF PASTRY

(Makes 18 large puffs or 40 small puffs)

1 cup water
½ cup butter
¾ cup whole wheat pastry flour
¼ cup gluten flour
4 eggs
½ teaspoon vanilla

Preheat oven to 425 degrees. In a saucepan, bring water and butter to a full boil. In a bowl, mix pastry flour and gluten flour with a wire whisk. Add flour mixture to boiling liquid and beat with a wooden spoon. Reduce heat to medium and continue beating until mixture forms a ball. Remove from heat and immediately beat in 1 egg at a time to form a glossy yellow dough. Beat in vanilla.

Spray baking sheets with non-stick vegetable spray and drop batter by tablespoons 3 inches apart for large puffs or by heaping teaspoons 1½ inches apart for small puffs. Bake in hot oven 40 minutes for large puffs or 20 minutes for small puffs until golden. Do not touch puffs, but turn oven off and allow puffs to stay in oven until they are completely cooled. This last step will prevent puffs from collapsing. Fill according to recipe directions.

3

Christmas-Hanukkah: A Holiday Season of Healthy Treats

GIFT-WRAPPED APPLES WITH VANILLA SAUCE
Serves 6

WRAPPED APPLE INGREDIENTS

Flaky Pastry Dough or Stretchy Pastry Dough recipe (see p. 16)

6 apples, peeled and cored

2 teaspoons cornstarch or arrowroot starch

½ cup raisins

2 tablespoons frozen apple juice concentrate, thawed

1 teaspoon grated orange peel

½ teaspoon cinnamon

1 egg yolk beaten with ½ teaspoon lemon juice

VANILLA SAUCE INGREDIENTS

3 eggs, lightly beaten

3 tablespoons frozen apple juice concentrate, thawed

1 tablespoon cornstarch

2½ cups milk

1 teaspoon vanilla

Preparation Time: 20 minutes
Baking Time: 40 minutes

Preheat oven to 425 degrees. Prepare pastry dough and divide into 6 balls. Roll into 8-inch circles. Trim and reserve trimmings. Place apples on circles.

In a bowl, mix cornstarch, raisins, apple juice concentrate, orange peel and cinnamon. Fill cavities of apples with mixture. Bring sides of dough circles over apples and press firmly. Gather at top and press to seal, then flatten. Turn apples upside down and place them on an oiled baking dish with gathered seam down. Brush with egg-yolk mixture. Roll leftover trimmings into a 6-inch-long rectangle and cut into 12 ½-inch strips with a pastry wheel. Crisscross two strips on the top of each apple, bringing them over the sides and pushing the ends under the apples. Brush strips with egg mixture. Bake apples for 40 minutes until golden brown.

While apples are baking, prepare sauce. Combine eggs, apple juice concentrate, cornstarch and milk in a double boiler. Cook, stirring occasionally, until thickened. Stir in vanilla and serve warm over apples.

Approximately 225 calories per serving
Approximately 30 grams carbohydrate per serving

CREAM PUFF CHRISTMAS TREE
Serves 16

CREAM PUFF AND FILLING INGREDIENTS

Cream Puff Pastry recipe (see p. 19)

¼ cup brown rice flour

2 cups frozen unsweetened strawberries, thawed

1 cup milk or skim milk

3 eggs, beaten

2 tablespoons frozen apple juice concentrate, thawed

GLAZE INGREDIENTS

1 tablespoon soft unsalted butter

½ cup carob powder

½ cup water

1 teaspoon vanilla

Preparation Time: 20 minutes
Baking Time: 1 hour
Assembling Time: 20 minutes

Preheat oven to 400 degrees. Prepare pastry and drop by teaspoons onto a baking sheet sprayed with vegetable spray. Bake for 30 minutes until puffed and golden. Turn off oven and leave puffs in oven to cool.

Prepare filling while puffs bake. Combine rice flour, strawberries with juice, milk, eggs and apple juice concentrate in a double boiler. Cook, stirring occasionally, until mixture thickens to a custard. Remove from heat and cool. Fill a pastry bag with mixture. When puffs are completely cooled make an inch-long slit in the side of each. Gently open by squeezing puff between fingers. Press filling from bag into puff.

To make glaze, combine butter, carob powder, water and vanilla in a saucepan. Heat, stirring occasionally, until sauce thickens. Remove from heat.

To assemble tree, cut a 9-inch circle of aluminum foil and place on a serving plate. Before setting each puff in place, dip bottom in glaze. Place puffs around the outer edge of foil circle. Fill the circle with puffs. Continue to make layers of slightly smaller circles with puffs to form a cone.

Just before serving, reheat sauce and pour over tree.

Approximately 225 calories per serving
Approximately 30 grams carbohydrate per serving

BAKED APPLE CHARLOTTE

Serves 15

CHARLOTTE INGREDIENTS

10 sweet apples, unpeeled,
cored and sliced
1 teaspoon butter
2 tablespoons frozen apple
juice concentrate, thawed
1 teaspoon cinnamon
1 tablespoon grated orange peel
2 tablespoons cider jelly
15 thin slices of stale whole
grain bread
2 egg yolks, beaten

SAUCE INGREDIENTS

1 cup fresh orange juice
1 tablespoon cornstarch
1 tablespoon sherry
2 teaspoons grated orange peel

Prepare apples. Melt butter in a heavy frying pan. Sauté apples until lightly browned. Stir in apple juice concentrate, cinnamon and orange peel. Cover and reduce heat. Cook until liquid has evaporated and then stir in jelly. Cook uncovered another 10 minutes to thicken.

Preheat oven to 450 degrees. Trim crusts from bread. Cut one slice of bread with a round cookie cutter. Place circle in the center of an oiled 6-cup soufflé dish. Cut 3 slices of bread into 4 triangles by slicing bread diagonally. Place overlapping triangles in two concentric circles around the circle of bread. Cut remaining slices of bread in half. Arrange 14 of these around the edge of the soufflé so that they extend slightly above the edge of the dish.

Beat egg yolks into apple purée, and turn into bread-lined soufflé. Cover top of soufflé with remaining bread halves. Cover with a circle of wax paper. Bake for 40 minutes. Carefully remove wax paper and cool for 90 minutes. With pastry scissors trim extended slices of bread. To unmold, carefully invert over a serving plate.

Preparation Time: 30 minutes
Baking Time: 40 to 45 minutes

Approximately 150 calories per serving
Over 35 grams carbohydrate per serving

CHRISTMAS APPLE CHEESE BREAD PUDDING

Serves 10

4 thin slices whole grain bread, quartered, with crusts removed
5 cups sliced apples
⅓ cup raisins
1 teaspoon cinnamon
2 tablespoons frozen apple juice concentrate, thawed
¼ cup apple juice
1 tablespoon cornstarch
¾ cup grated Cheddar cheese

Preparation Time: 10 minutes
Baking Time: 50 Minutes

Preheat oven to 350 degrees. Line oiled 9 x 12-inch baking dish with bread. Combine apples, raisins, cinnamon, apple juice concentrate, apple juice and cornstarch. Pour over bread. Bake, covered, for 30 minutes, until apples are tender. Sprinkle with cheese and continue baking, uncovered, for 20 minutes until cheese is completely melted. This dish is best served hot.

Approximately 150 calories per serving
Under 30 grams carbohydrate per serving

PLUM PIE WITH CHESTNUT SAUCE

Serves 8

PIE INGREDIENTS
Flaky Pastry Dough or Stretchy Pastry Dough recipe (see p. 16)
4 cups pitted, sliced plums
3 tablespoons frozen apple juice concentrate, thawed
3 tablespoons cornstarch
3 tablespoons currants

SAUCE INGREDIENTS
½ cup sifted chestnut flour
2 cups apple cider

Preheat oven to 400 degrees. Divide dough into two portions. Roll into 2 12-inch circles. Line pie plate with one circle. In a bowl, toss plums, apple juice concentrate, cornstarch and currants until well combined. Pour into lined pie plate and cover with second crust. Trim and flute edges. Prick top with a fork so that steam may escape. Bake for 50 minutes or until lightly browned.

While pie bakes, prepare sauce. Place chestnut flour in a heated heavy skillet and dry-roast until lightly toasted. In a saucepan, combine roasted flour, apple cider, tahini and cardamom. Cook over medium heat, stirring occasionally, for 15 minutes until mix-

2 tablespoons tahini
½ teaspoon ground cardamom
1 teaspoon vanilla

Preparation Time: 20 minutes
Baking Time: 50 minutes
Assembling Time: 15 minutes

ture thickens. Remove from heat and stir in vanilla. Serve with warm pie.

Approximately 150 calories per serving
Approximately 30 grams carbohydrate per serving

APPLE PLUM COBBLER *Serves 9*

FILLING INGREDIENTS
2 cups pitted, chopped plums
2 cups cored, sliced apples
3 tablespoons frozen apple
   juice concentrate, thawed
2 tablespoons cornstarch

TOPPING INGREDIENTS
1 cup whole wheat pastry flour
1½ teaspoons baking powder
⅓ cup soft butter
2 tablespoons frozen apple
   juice concentrate, thawed
1 tablespoon water

Preparation Time: 20 minutes
Baking Time: 30 to 40 minutes

Preheat oven to 375 degrees. In a bowl, toss plums, apples, apple juice concentrate and cornstarch until thoroughly combined. Pour into an 8-inch square baking dish. In another bowl, combine flour and baking powder. Cut in butter to form a mixture with the consistency of coarse meal. Stir in apple juice concentrate and water to form a dough. Drop flour mixture by spoonfuls onto fruit mixture. Bake for 30 to 40 minutes until lightly browned.

Approximately 150 calories per serving
Over 35 grams carbohydrate per serving

CRANBERRY CHRISTMAS CHEESECAKE

Serves 12 to 16

CHEESECAKE INGREDIENTS

Crumble Crust recipe (see p. 17)
3 eggs, separated
⅔ cup frozen apple juice concentrate, thawed
2 teaspoons vanilla
1½ cups cottage cheese
1½ cups part skim milk ricotta cheese
2 tablespoons soy flour
1 tablespoon grated orange peel

TOPPING INGREDIENTS

1 cup cranberries
3 tablespoons frozen apple juice concentrate, thawed
1 cup apple juice
1 tablespoon grated orange peel
2 tablespoons cornstarch or arrowroot starch, mixed with 1 tablespoon water

Preparation Time: 15 minutes
Baking Time: 1 hour
Assembling Time: 10 minutes

Preheat oven to 400 degrees. Line a 10-inch springform pan with crumble crust. Bake for 10 minutes until lightly browned and remove from oven to cool.

In an electric blender, combine egg yolks, apple juice concentrate, vanilla, cottage cheese, ricotta, soy flour and orange peel. Blend until smooth. Beat egg whites until stiff and fold into cheesecake batter. Pour into the lined springform pan. Reduce oven to 350 degrees and bake for 1 hour until a knife inserted into the center of the cake comes out clean.

While cake bakes, prepare topping. In a saucepan, combine cranberries, apple juice concentrate, apple juice and orange peel. Cook over medium heat until cranberries begin to pop. With a potato masher, crush cranberries. Continue cooking and stir in starch-and-water mixture. Cook, stirring occasionally, until mixture thickens. Remove from heat. Spread cranberry topping evenly over cheesecake. Cool 10 minutes. Run a knife between cake and springform. Remove springform. Cool completely before serving.

Approximately 225 calories per serving
Approximately 30 grams carbohydrate per serving

CRANBERRY CHRISTMAS PIE

Serves 8

Flaky Pastry Dough or Stretchy Pastry Dough recipe (see p. 16)

3 cups cranberries

⅓ cup chopped walnuts

2 teaspoons grated orange peel

¼ cup quick-cooking tapioca

⅓ cup frozen apple juice concentrate, thawed

Preparation Time: 20 minutes
Baking Time: 50 minutes
Cooling Time: 2 hours

Preheat oven to 450 degrees. Roll dough into 2 12-inch circles. Line pie plate with one circle. In a bowl, combine cranberries, walnuts, orange peel, tapioca and apple juice concentrate. Allow mixture to stand for 10 minutes. Pour into lined pie plate. Cover with top crust, trim and flute edges. Prick top crust with a fork to allow steam to escape. Bake for 10 minutes. Reduce heat to 350 and bake for 40 minutes until golden brown. Cool at least 2 hours before serving.

Approximately 150 calories per serving
Approximately 30 grams carbohydrate per serving

RAISIN NUT MOUSSE

Serves 8 to 10

⅔ cup raisins

⅔ cup apple juice

2 envelopes unflavored gelatin

4 eggs, separated

3 cups milk

4 tablespoons cornstarch

2 teaspoons grain coffee substitute

1 teaspoon vanilla

½ cup chopped walnuts

2 teaspoons apple cider jelly

Preparation Time: 30 minutes
Chilling Time: 4 hours

In a saucepan, heat raisins and apple juice to boiling. Remove from heat and stir in gelatin. Set aside.

In another saucepan, combine egg yolks, milk, cornstarch, coffee substitute, vanilla, walnuts and cider jelly. Cook over medium heat, stirring occasionally, until thickened. Remove from heat and stir in raisin and apple juice mixture. Chill until mixture resembles custard but is not set, about 40 minutes.

Beat egg whites until stiff and glossy. Fold into chilled mixture. Pour into a 6-cup gelatin mold and refrigerate for 3 to 3½ hours until firm. Unmold to serve.

Approximately 225 calories per serving
Approximately 30 grams carbohydrate per serving

INDIVIDUAL APPLE SOUFFLÉS

Serves 6

2 cups unsweetened applesauce

2 tablespoons frozen apple
 juice concentrate, thawed

2 teaspoons grated orange peel

4 egg whites

Preheat oven to 350 degrees. In a bowl, combine applesauce, apple juice concentrate and orange peel. Spoon 1 tablespoon of mixture into 6 individual custard cups. Beat egg whites until stiff and glossy. Fold into remaining applesauce mixture. Spoon into custard cups. Bake for 15 to 20 minutes until golden. Serve immediately.

Preparation Time: 10 minutes
Baking Time: 15 to 20 minutes

Under 150 calories per serving
Under 30 grams carbohydrate per serving

FLOATING ISLANDS

Serves 12

CUSTARD INGREDIENTS

2½ cups milk

8 egg yolks, beaten

¼ cup frozen apple juice concentrate, thawed

1 teaspoon cornstarch

2 teaspoons vanilla

MERINGUE INGREDIENTS

2 tablespoons liquid barley
 malt

2 tablespoons water

8 egg whites, at room temperature

1 teaspoon vanilla

1 teaspoon cinnamon

In a saucepan, combine milk, egg yolks, apple juice concentrate and cornstarch. Cook over medium heat, stirring occasionally, until mixture thickens enough to coat spoon and until there is no taste of starch. Pour into a shallow 9 x 12 x 2-inch dish and chill for 1 hour.

To make meringues, heat malt and water to boiling. Boil for 10 minutes until mixture reaches soft-ball stage. Beat egg whites until foamy. Gradually drizzle in malt mixture while continuing to beat. Add vanilla and cinnamon. When whites are stiff and glossy, bring 2 inches of water to a simmer in a shallow covered pan. Gently spoon 12 meringues onto water and simmer for 2 to 3 minutes until set. Remove from water with a slotted spatula and place on custard, just before serving.

Preparation Time: 10 minutes
Chilling Time: 1 hour
Assembling Time: 10 minutes

Approximately 150 calories per serving
Approximately 20 grams carbohydrate per serving

APPLE MINCE CRUMB PIE

Serves 8

1 cup chopped dates
1 cup water
3 cups finely chopped unpeeled
   apples
1 tablespoon apple cider jelly
1 teaspoon cinnamon
½ teaspoon ground ginger
½ teaspoon ground cloves
⅛ teaspoon ground nutmeg
3 tablespoons apple juice
2 tablespoons frozen orange
   juice concentrate, thawed
1 tablespoon grated orange peel
3 tablespoons butter
1 tablespoon cornstarch

½ Flaky Pastry Dough recipe
   (see p. 16)
⅔ cup sugarless cake or cookie
   crumbs
1 tablespoon melted butter

In a saucepan, combine dates, water, apples, cider jelly, cinnamon, ginger, cloves, nutmeg, apple juice, orange juice concentrate, orange peel and butter. Cook over medium heat until mixture forms a thick sauce. Remove from heat and stir in cornstarch.

Prepare pie dough and line pie plate. Pour filling into plate. Preheat oven to 375 degrees. In a small bowl, toss crumbs with melted butter. Sprinkle over pie and bake for 50 minutes until crust and crumbs are lightly browned.

Preparation Time: 25 minutes
Baking Time: 50 minutes

Approximately 150 calories per serving
Under 30 grams carbohydrate per serving

TAPIOCA PLUM PARFAITS

Serves 6 to 8

TAPIOCA INGREDIENTS
¼ cup quick-cooking tapioca
1¾ cups milk
3 tablespoons frozen apple

In a saucepan, combine tapioca, milk, apple juice concentrate and egg yolks. Cook, stirring constantly, for 15 minutes until mixture thickens. Stir in almond extract and refrigerate for 2 hours until set.

juice concentrate, thawed
3 eggs, separated
½ teaspoon almond extract

PLUM SAUCE INGREDIENTS
1½ cups pitted prunes, halved
1 cup apple juice
⅓ cup raisins
½ teaspoon cinnamon
1 teaspoon grated orange peel
Preparation Time: 25 minutes
Chilling Time: 2 hours
Assembling Time: 10 minutes

While tapioca chills, prepare plum sauce. In a saucepan, combine prunes, apple juice, raisins, cinnamon and grated orange peel. Cook over medium heat until prunes are tender. Place in an electric blender or food processor and purée until smooth. Refrigerate to cool. Beat 3 egg whites until stiff and glossy. Fold into tapioca. Alternate layers of tapioca and plum sauce in parfait glasses before serving.

Approximately 150 calories per serving
Under 30 grams carbohydrate per serving

ENGLISH CHRISTMAS TRIFLE

Serves 10

Half stale Lemon Loaf (see p. 102), cut in 1-inch cubes
SAUCE INGREDIENTS
⅓ cup frozen unsweetened strawberries or raspberries, thawed
2 tablespoons frozen apple juice concentrate, thawed
1 teaspoon cornstarch

CUSTARD INGREDIENTS
2 cups milk
3 egg yolks
1 tablespoon cornstarch
2 tablespoons frozen apple juice concentrate, thawed

Prepare cake cubes and set aside. To prepare sauce, combine strawberries or raspberries, apple juice concentrate and cornstarch in a saucepan. Cook over medium heat, stirring occasionally, until sauce thickens. Remove from heat and set aside.

In another saucepan, combine milk, egg yolks, cornstarch, apple juice concentrate and vanilla. Cook, stirring occasionally, without bringing to a boil, until mixture thickens. Set aside to cool.

Prepare whipped cream by adding apple juice concentrate and vanilla to cream and beating until stiff.

Have sauce, custard, whipped cream, sherry and fruit within easy reach to begin assembling trifle. In a 2-quart glass bowl, place a layer of cake cubes, using half the cubes. Pour sauce over cubes. Place remaining cake over sauce. Pour sherry over both layers of cake and sauce. Allow to marinate 15 minutes. Spoon

1 teaspoon vanilla

WHIPPED CREAM
INGREDIENTS
1 cup heavy cream
1 tablespoon frozen apple juice
concentrate, thawed
½ teaspoon vanilla

ASSEMBLING INGREDIENTS
⅔ cup sherry
2 cups canned or frozen unsweetened fruit, drained and
thawed

Preparation and Assembling
Time: 45 minutes

fruit over marinated cake. Spoon custard over fruit and top with whipped cream.

Over 250 calories per serving
Over 35 grams carbohydrate per serving

HANUKKAH YOGURT CHEESE PANCAKES   *Serves 6 to 8*

1 cup 2% cottage cheese
½ cup yogurt
3 eggs, beaten
1 teaspoon vanilla
2 tablespoons frozen apple
juice concentrate, thawed
⅓ cup whole wheat pastry flour
⅓ cup brown rice flour
½ teaspoon baking powder
1½ cups unsweetened applesauce

Preparation Time: 10 minutes
Frying Time: 15 minutes

In a bowl, mix cottage cheese, yogurt, eggs, vanilla and apple juice concentrate. In a separate bowl, beat pastry flour, rice flour and baking powder with a wire whisk. Gradually mix dry ingredients into liquids to form a batter.

Heat a lightly oiled heavy griddle or skillet over medium-high heat. Drop batter by spoonfuls onto griddle. When bubbles cover the surface of each pancake turn to brown second side. Serve with applesauce.

Approximately 225 calories per serving
Over 35 grams carbohydrate per serving

DESSERT LATKES

Serves 8 to 10

5 potatoes, grated
1 onion, grated
2 eggs, beaten
2 tablespoons whole wheat
  pastry flour
½ teaspoon cinnamon
½ cup oil, for frying
1 cup part-skim milk ricotta
  cheese
1 tablespoon frozen apple juice
  concentrate, thawed
1 cup unsweetened applesauce

Preparation Time: 20 minutes
Frying Time: 25 minutes

With a wooden spoon mix grated potato, grated onion, eggs, flour and cinnamon. Heat oil in a heavy frying pan to 375 degrees or until water sizzles when sprinkled on it. Form potato mixture into patties and fry until both sides are golden brown and crisp.

In an electric blender or food processor, blend ricotta and apple juice concentrate until smooth. Serve latkes topped with applesauce and ricotta mixture.

Over 250 calories per serving
Over 35 grams carbohydrate per serving

HANUKKAH DESSERT BLINTZES

Serves 15 to 20

Delicate Whole Wheat Crêpes
  or Low Calorie Eggless
  Crêpes recipe (see p. 18)

FILLING INGREDIENTS
2 cups 2% cottage cheese
2 tablespoons frozen apple
  juice concentrate, thawed
1 teaspoon vanilla
½ teaspoon cinnamon

Prepare crêpes according to instructions on p. 18. To make filling, combine cottage cheese, apple juice concentrate, vanilla and cinnamon. Place a line of filling down the center of each crêpe and fold both sides over filling. Arrange in a covered ovenproof dish and keep warm in the oven at 200 degrees.

In a saucepan, combine apple juice or cider, cinnamon, grated orange peel and cornstarch. Heat, stirring occasionally, until mixture thickens to a light sauce. Pour over blintzes just before serving.

SAUCE INGREDIENTS

2 cups apple juice or cider

1 teaspoon cinnamon

1 tablespoon grated orange peel

2 teaspoons cornstarch

Preparation Time: 20 minutes
Cooking Time: 25 minutes
Assembling Time: 10 minutes

Approximately 150 calories per serving
Approximately 30 grams carbohydrate per serving

STEAMED BANANA PUDDING with Cranberry Sauce   *Serves 10*

PUDDING INGREDIENTS

2 cups mashed ripe bananas

2½ cups sugarless cake or
cookie crumbs

¾ cup frozen pineapple juice
concentrate, thawed

⅓ cup melted butter

2 eggs, lightly beaten

3 tablespoons whole wheat
pastry flour

2 teaspoons baking powder

¾ teaspoon cinnamon

½ teaspoon ground ginger

SAUCE INGREDIENTS

1 cup cranberries

3 tablespoons frozen apple
juice concentrate, thawed

1½ cups apple juice

Combine all pudding ingredients and spoon into a well-oiled 6-cup metal mold. Cover mold with a double layer of foil and tie with a string. Place a rack in a covered pot large enough to hold mold. Fill pot with enough boiling water to cover halfway up the mold. Cover pot and boil for 4 hours until a knife inserted into the center of the pudding comes out clean. (When necessary pour additional boiling water into pot.) Unmold to serve.

To make sauce, combine cranberries, apple juice concentrate and apple juice in a saucepan. Cook over medium heat until cranberries pop. Stir in cornstarch-and-orange-juice mixture to thicken cranberry mixture. Remove from heat and serve warm with pudding.

2 tablespoons cornstarch dissolved in 1 tablespoon frozen
orange juice concentrate,
thawed

Preparation Time: 15 minutes
Steaming Time: 4 hours
Assembling Time: 20 minutes

Approximately 225 calories per serving
Over 35 grams carbohydrate per serving

STUFFED PLUMS

Serves 20 to 25

1 12-ounce box large pitted
prunes
½ cup cashew butter
¼ cup unsweetened shredded
coconut

Preparation Time: 25 minutes

With a sharp knife cut small slits in prunes. In a bowl
mix cashew butter and coconut until well combined.
Spoon mixture into the opening of each prune.

To give as a gift, place stuffed plums in one layer in
a decorative Christmas box.

Approximately 150 calories per serving
Approximately 30 grams carbohydrate per serving

STUFFED DATES

Serves 15

15 large soft pitted dates
¼ cup unsweetened shredded
coconut
15 whole almonds

Preparation Time: 20 minutes

Roll dates in coconut. Insert almond into cavities.

When placed almond side up in a decorative
Christmas-Hanukkah box, these dates make a delicious gift.

Approximately 150 calories per serving
Approximately 30 grams carbohydrate per serving

APPLE BUTTER

Makes 4 to 6 cups

15 cups peeled, cored and chopped apples
½ cup water
1 tablespoon cinnamon
1 tablespoon finely grated orange peel

Preparation Time: 20 minutes
Cooking Time: 3 to 5 hours

Place all ingredients in a large covered pot. Cook over low heat for 1 hour until sauce forms. Remove cover and continue to cook, stirring every 10 minutes until a thick brown butter is formed.

Placed in decorative 1-cup jars and tied with a ribbon, apple butter makes a welcome Christmas or Hanukkah present.

Low Calorie-Moderate Carbohydrate

CAROB COCONUT COOKIES

Makes 1½ dozen

1 cup unsweetened shredded coconut
1 egg, separated
4 teaspoons roasted carob powder
3 teaspoons apple juice

Preparation Time: 10 minutes
Baking Time: 15 minutes

Preheat oven to 300 degrees. In a bowl, combine coconut, egg yolk, carob powder and apple juice. Beat egg white until stiff and glossy. Fold into coconut-carob mixture. Drop by spoonfuls onto a cookie sheet sprayed with non-stick vegetable spray. Bake for 15 minutes or until edges are lightly browned.

As gifts, these cookies can be placed in a decorative cookie jar or tin alone or with other festive cookies.

Under 150 calories per serving
Under 20 grams carbohydrate per serving

SHERRIED MACAROON BALLS

Makes 1 dozen

1 cup unsweetened shredded
  coconut
3 tablespoons sherry
1 tablespoon non-instant skim
  milk powder
2 egg whites

Preheat oven to 325 degrees. In a bowl, combine coconut, sherry and milk powder. Beat egg whites until stiff and glossy. Fold into coconut-sherry mixture. Drop by spoonfuls onto a baking sheet sprayed with non-stick vegetable spray. Bake for 20 minutes until edges are lightly browned. Cool.

Place in a decorative jar or container alone or with other cookies as a festive holiday season gift.

Preparation Time: 10 minutes
Baking Time: 20 minutes

Under 150 calories per serving
Under 30 grams carbohydrate per serving

BABY WALNUT DATE TARTS

Makes 2 to 3 dozen

2 tablespoons frozen apple
  juice concentrate, thawed
1 tablespoon melted butter
1 cup chopped walnuts
¼ cup finely chopped dates
2 eggs, beaten
Stretchy Pastry Dough recipe
  (see p. 16)

In a bowl, mix apple juice concentrate, butter, walnuts, dates and eggs.

Roll dough in a large rectangle. Cut into 2-inch circles using a glass or cookie cutter. Pinch sides of circles to form a ¼-inch edge. Spoon a small amount of filling into each small tart. Place on an oiled baking sheet.

Preheat oven to 325 degrees and bake for 20 minutes until lightly browned. Cool.

Place in a decorative tin alone or with other cookies if these festive tarts are to be used as holiday gifts

Preparation Time: 25 minutes
Baking Time: 20 minutes

Approximately 225 calories per serving
Approximately 20 grams carbohydrate per serving

PINWHEELS

Makes 3 dozen

LIGHT DOUGH INGREDIENTS

1½ cups whole wheat pastry
   flour
2 tablespoons gluten flour
1 tablespoon grated orange peel
¾ cup soft unsalted butter
4 tablespoons frozen apple
   juice concentrate, thawed
3 teaspoons vanilla
1 egg, beaten

DARK DOUGH INGREDIENTS

¾ cup whole wheat pastry flour
¾ cup roasted carob powder
⅔ cup soft unsalted butter
3 tablespoons ice water
3 teaspoons vanilla
1 egg, beaten

Preparation Time: 1½ to 2 hours
Chilling Time: Overnight
Baking Time: 12 minutes

To make light dough, mix pastry flour and gluten flour. Stir in orange peel. Cut in butter to form coarse meal. Stir in apple juice concentrate, vanilla and egg to form a firm dough. Refrigerate.

To make dark dough, combine flour and carob powder. Cut in butter to form coarse meal. Stir in ice water, vanilla and egg to form a stiff dough. Refrigerate. If either dough is too sticky, add more flour. If too dry, add more water. Chill for 1 hour until firm.

Roll each dough separately into a 12 x 16-inch rectangle. Place dark dough on top of light dough. With a sharp knife, cut in 4-inch strips. Roll along long edge in jelly roll fashion. Wrap rolls in waxed paper and refrigerate overnight.

Preheat oven to 350 degrees. Slice rolls ¼-inch thick and place on oiled baking sheets. Bake for 10 to 12 minutes until lightly browned.

For holiday gifts, arrange in decorative tins or cookie jars alone or with other cookies.

Under 150 calories per serving
Under 30 grams carbohydrate per serving

JOE FROGGERS

Makes 3 dozen

4 cups whole wheat pastry flour
2 cups chestnut flour
1 cup raw wheat germ

In a bowl, combine pastry flour, chestnut flour, raw wheat germ, cinnamon, ginger, baking powder and cloves. Add oil to form a coarse meal. Stir in apple

1 tablespoon cinnamon
1 tablespoon ground ginger
2 teaspoons baking powder
½ teaspoon ground cloves
¾ cup safflower or sunflower oil
½ cup frozen apple juice concentrate, thawed
3 tablespoons blackstrap molasses
1 cup apple cider or apple juice

Preparation Time: 15 minutes
Baking Time: 12 to 15 minutes

juice concentrate, molasses and cider or apple juice to form a thick batter. If batter is too stiff, add more juice. If too moist, add flour.

Preheat oven to 375 degrees. Drop batter in tablespoon-size mounds, well spaced on oiled baking sheets. Bake for 10 to 15 minutes until edges are lightly browned. Cool.

As holiday gifts, place in stacks of six, wrap in colored cellophane or foil, and tie with a bow.

Approximately 150 calories per serving
Over 35 grams carbohydrate per serving

LEMON ALMOND SANDWICH CRÈME COOKIES   *Makes 3 dozen*

COOKIE DOUGH INGREDIENTS
½ cup oil
1 teaspoon vanilla
¼ cup frozen apple juice concentrate, thawed
2 teaspoons lemon juice
1 tablespoon grated lemon peel
1 cup chestnut flour or soy flour
2 tablespoons gluten flour
2 cups whole wheat pastry flour
1 teaspoon baking powder
1 teaspoon cinnamon

FILLING INGREDIENTS
1 cup almond butter

To make dough, mix oil, vanilla, apple juice concentrate, lemon juice and lemon peel in one bowl. In a second bowl, combine chestnut flour or soy flour, gluten flour, pastry flour, baking powder and cinnamon. Gradually add dry ingredients to liquid to form a firm dough. If necessary, add more flour or water to reach proper consistency. Cover and chill for 1 hour until firm.

Preheat oven to 350 degrees. Roll dough ⅛-inch thick. Cut into circles using the bottom of a glass or cookie cutter. Place circles on an oiled baking sheet and bake for 10 minutes until lightly browned. Remove from oven and cool.

To make filling, combine almond butter, apple juice concentrate, lemon juice and lemon peel. Spread a thin layer of filling over half of wafers. Cover with other wafers to create small round sandwich cookies.

3 tablespoons frozen apple
  juice concentrate, thawed
2 tablespoons lemon juice
1 tablespoon grated lemon peel

Preparation Time: 15 minutes
Chilling Time: 1 hour
Baking Time: 10 minutes
Assembling Time: 15 minutes

As holiday gifts, place in a decorative container, alone or with other cookies.

Approximately 225 calories per serving
Over 35 grams carbohydrate per serving

CAROB MINT SANDWICH COOKIES

Makes 2 dozen

CAROB COOKIE DOUGH IN-
GREDIENTS
¼ cup strong peppermint tea,
  cooled
¼ cup oil
¼ cup frozen apple juice concentrate, thawed
1½ cups roasted carob powder
1½ cups whole wheat pastry
  flour

FILLING INGREDIENTS
¼ cup soft unsalted butter
1 cup non-instant milk powder
⅓ cup carob powder
⅔ cup strong peppermint tea

Preparation Time: 10 minutes
Chilling Time: 1 hour
Baking Time: 10 minutes
Assembling Time: 20 minutes

To make cookie dough, mix tea, oil and apple juice concentrate. In a separate bowl, mix carob powder and pastry flour. Gradually stir dry ingredients into liquids to form a stiff dough. Refrigerate for 1 hour until chilled.

Preheat oven to 350 degrees. Form dough into teaspoon-size balls. Place on well-oiled baking sheets 2 inches apart and press into circles with the bottom of a dampened tumbler. Bake for 10 minutes. Cool.

To make filling, combine butter, milk powder, carob powder and tea in an electric blender or food processor until smooth and thick. Spread filling on half of carob cookies. Cover with other half.

These cookies make wonderful gifts when placed in decorative containers alone or with other festive cookies.

Under 150 calories per serving
Approximately 30 grams carbohydrate per serving

DATE-FILLED COOKIES

Makes 3 dozen

DOUGH INGREDIENTS
2 cups whole wheat pastry flour
2 tablespoons gluten flour
1 cup soft unsalted butter
1 teaspoon vanilla
5 to 6 tablespoons frozen apple
  juice concentrate, thawed

FILLING INGREDIENTS
1 cup chopped dates
1 cup water
½ cup chopped walnuts
1 tablespoon grated orange peel

Preparation Time: 15 minutes
Chilling Time: 1 hour
Assembling Time: 20 minutes
Baking Time: 15 to 20 minutes

In a bowl, combine whole wheat pastry flour and gluten flour with a wire whisk. Cut in butter to form a coarse meal. Stir in vanilla and apple juice concentrate, 1 tablespoon at a time, to form ball. Wrap in waxed paper and chill for 1 hour.

While dough chills, make filling. In a saucepan, combine dates and water. Cook over medium heat until a thick sauce forms. Remove from heat and stir in nuts and orange peel. Roll dough thin on a board floured with cornstarch. Cut into 2-inch circles with a cookie cutter. Place 1 teaspoon of filling in the center of half of circles. Cover with the other half and seal with the prongs of a fork dipped in water.

Preheat oven to 350 degrees. Bake for 15 to 20 minutes until edges are lightly browned. Cool.

These festive cookies make welcome holiday gifts when placed in decorative tins, alone or with other fancy cookies.

Approximately 150 calories per serving
Over 35 grams carbohydrate per serving

ALMOND DROPS

Makes 3 dozen

3 egg whites
2 tablespoons frozen apple
  juice concentrate, thawed
1 teaspoon grated orange peel
1⅔ cups ground almonds

Preheat oven to 325 degrees. Beat egg whites until foamy. Continue to beat, gradually adding apple juice concentrate. Beat until firm, about 15 minutes. Combine orange peel and almonds and fold into egg-white mixture. Fill pastry bag with mixture and press drops onto a baking sheet sprayed with non-stick vegetable spray. Bake for 10 to 15 minutes until lightly browned. Cool.

Placed in a decorative container alone or with other festive cookies, Almond Drops make a welcome holiday gift.

Preparation Time: 15 minutes
Baking Time: 10 to 15 minutes

Approximately 150 calories per serving
Approximately 20 grams carbohydrate per serving

DELICATE ORANGE COOKIES

Makes 3 dozen

¼ cup soft unsalted butter
1¾ cups non-instant skim milk powder
⅔ cup orange juice
1 tablespoon grated orange peel
½ teaspoon cinnamon

Preheat oven to 325 degrees. In an electric blender or food processor, mix butter, milk powder, orange juice, orange peel and cinnamon. Drop batter by teaspoonfuls onto an oiled baking sheet. Bake for 10 minutes or until lightly browned.

Arrange in a decorative box alone or with other cookies.

Preparation Time: 10 minutes
Baking Time: 10 minutes

Under 150 calories per serving
Under 20 grams carbohydrate per serving

FRUIT CAKE

Makes 3 loaves; each serves 15 to 20

2 pounds mixed dried fruit, chopped
4½ cups hard cider
4 eggs, beaten
¾ cup oil
3 cups whole wheat pastry flour
2 cups raw wheat germ
1 tablespoon baking powder

Place fruit in cider and allow to stand overnight. Preheat oven to 350 degrees. Mix eggs and oil into fruit mixture.

In a separate bowl, combine pastry flour, wheat germ, baking powder and cinnamon. Gradually stir flour mixture into fruit mixture to form a batter. Stir in orange peel and 1 cup walnuts. Pour batter into 3 well-oiled loaf pans. Place 5 whole walnuts on each

4 teaspoons cinnamon

2 tablespoons grated orange
   peel

1 cup coarsely chopped walnuts

15 whole walnuts

*Preparation Time: Overnight plus
15 minutes*
Baking Time: 90 minutes

loaf. Bake for about 90 minutes until done. Cool 10 minutes. Remove from pans and cool on racks.

Wrapped in foil or cellophane and decorated with a bow, these loaves make lovely gifts

Under 225 calories per serving
Over 35 grams carbohydrate per serving

SWEDISH TEA RING

Makes 3 12-inch rings; each serves 12

DOUGH INGREDIENTS

2 tablespoons baking yeast

2 cups warm apple juice

3 tablespoons melted butter

2 eggs, beaten

½ cup frozen apple juice concentrate, thawed

2 teaspoons ground cardamom

4½ cups whole wheat pastry
   flour

1½ cups soy flour

1½ cups gluten flour

FILLING INGREDIENTS

¾ cup whole wheat pastry flour

2 tablespoons cinnamon

1 teaspoon ground nutmeg

2 tablespoons grated orange
   peel

In a bowl, sprinkle yeast over warm apple juice. Allow to stand 10 minutes until yeast dissolves. Stir in melted butter, eggs and apple juice concentrate.

In a separate bowl, mix cardamom, pastry flour, soy flour and gluten flour. Gradually beat 2½ cups of flour mixture into liquids. Cover and let rise in a warm place for 20 minutes until a sponge forms. Beat in remaining flour mixture to form a dough. Knead for 10 minutes until smooth and elastic. If dough becomes sticky, knead in additional flour. Form into a ball, oil and place in a bowl. Cover with a warm damp towel and let rise in a warm place for 1 to 1½ hours until doubled. Punch down and divide dough into 3 equal portions. Roll each portion on a floured surface to 12 ⁃ 5-inch rectangle. Cover with towels and prepare filling.

In a bowl, combine flour, cinnamon, nutmeg and orange peel. Cut in butter to form a coarse meal. Stir in pecans. Remove towels from dough and brush with melted butter. Sprinkle a third of filling mixture evenly

⅔ cup butter
1 cup chopped pecans
2 tablespoons melted butter

GLAZE INGREDIENTS
¼ cup soft butter
1½ cups non-instant skim milk
    powder
½ cup pineapple juice
1 teaspoon vanilla

GARNISH
2 tablespoons chopped pecans

Preparation and Rising Time:
3 hours
Baking Time: 30 minutes
Glazing Time: 5 minutes

over 3 rectangles. Roll in jelly roll fashion along 15-inch edge. Place seam sides down on oiled baking sheets. Bring ends together to form 3 rings. Pinch ends to seal. With pastry scissors, cut from the outside of rings almost to the center about 1½ inches apart to form serving pieces. Cover and let rise in a warm place for about 1 hour until doubled.

Preheat oven to 325 degrees. Bake for 30 minutes until lightly browned. If rings become overbrown cover with foil for the last 10 minutes of baking. Place on wire racks to cool.

To make glaze, beat butter, milk powder, pineapple juice and vanilla in an electric blender or food processor until smooth. Drizzle over rings while still slightly warm. Sprinkle with chopped pecans.

These make delicious gifts if placed in decorative tins or wrapped in colored cellophane and tied with bows when completely cool. For a fresh-baked texture, these gifts can be wrapped in foil and reheated at 300 degrees just before serving.

Approximately 150 calories per serving
Over 35 grams carbohydrate per serving

ENGLISH PLUM PUDDING

Serves 16 to 20

½ cup whole wheat pastry flour
½ cup brown rice flour
1 teaspoon baking soda
1 teaspoon baking powder
1 teaspoon cinnamon
¾ teaspoon mace
¼ teaspoon nutmeg

In a large bowl, mix flours, baking soda, baking powder, cinnamon, mace, nutmeg, currants, raisins, grated orange peel, walnuts and bread crumbs.

In a separate bowl, cream butter, eggs, cider jelly and apple juice concentrate.

Gradually stir dry mixture into liquids. Pour into a well-oiled heat-proof 2-quart mold. Cover with a dou-

2 cups currants
1½ cups raisins
2 tablespoons grated orange
  peel
½ cup chopped walnuts
1½ cups soft whole grain bread
  crumbs
½ cup soft butter
3 eggs, beaten
⅓ cup cider jelly
¼ cup frozen apple juice concentrate, thawed

Preparation Time: 15 minutes
Steaming Time: 4 hours

ble layer of foil and tie with string. Place on a rack in a large covered pot. Pour boiling water halfway up the side of the mold. Cover and steam for 4 hours. Replace water as it evaporates. Remove from steamer only when a knife inserted into the center of the pudding comes out clean. Unmold pudding and set on a rack to cool.

English plum pudding makes a traditional holiday gift if placed in a decorative tin or wrapped with foil and tied with a bow.

Approximately 225 calories per serving
Over 35 grams carbohydrate per serving

SPICED WINE

Serves 10

1 3-inch cinnamon stick
1 teaspoon whole cloves
1 ¼-inch ginger root
⅓ cup raisins
¼ cup frozen apple juice concentrate, thawed
1 cup white grape juice
3 cups dry wine
¼ cup slivered almonds

Preparation Time: 10 minutes
Cooking Time: 40 minutes

Tie cinnamon, cloves and ginger root in a cheesecloth. Place in a large enamel pot. Add raisins, apple juice concentrate and grape juice. Cover and simmer for 10 minutes. Add wine and cook on low heat for 30 minutes. Ladle into cups and sprinkle with almonds.

Under 150 calories per serving
Over 35 grams carbohydrate per serving

MULLED CIDER

Serves 12

6 cups cider
4 3-inch cinnamon sticks
10 cloves

Preparation and Cooking Time:
30 minutes

Place all ingredients in a pot and simmer for 30 minutes before serving.

Under 150 calories per serving
Under 30 grams carbohydrate per serving

SWEDISH GLOGG

Serves 10

10 whole cardamom pods
3 1-inch strips orange peel
5 whole cloves
1 3-inch cinnamon stick
1 tablespoon fennel seeds
½ cup slivered almonds
½ cup raisins
3½ cups dry red wine
1½ cups aquavit

Preparation and Cooking Time:
35 minutes

Place cardamom, orange peel, cloves, cinnamon stick and fennel seeds in cheesecloth, tie and place in a large enamel pot. Add almonds, raisins and wine. Heat over low heat for 30 minutes. Add aquavit just before serving.

Approximately 150 calories per serving
Over 35 grams carbohydrate per serving

Children's Christmas or Hanukkah Treats

GINGERBREAD CHARACTERS

Serves 12

DOUGH INGREDIENTS

1 tablespoon baking yeast
1 cup warm apple juice
2 tablespoons melted butter
1 egg, beaten
3 tablespoons blackstrap molasses
1 teaspoon cinnamon
1 teaspoon ground ginger
2¼ cups whole wheat pastry flour
¾ cup soy flour
¾ cup gluten flour

DECORATING INGREDIENTS

Raisins
Almonds
1 egg beaten with 1 tablespoon frozen apple juice concentrate, thawed

Preparation and Rising Time: 3 hours
Baking Time: 25 minutes

In a large bowl, sprinkle yeast over warm apple juice. Let stand 10 minutes until dissolved. Stir in butter, beaten egg and molasses. In a separate bowl, combine cinnamon, ginger, pastry flour, soy flour and gluten flour. Beat 1½ cups of flour mixture into liquids. Cover and let rise in a warm place for 20 minutes. Beat in remaining flour mixture to form a soft dough. Knead on a floured board for 10 minutes until smooth and elastic. If dough becomes sticky, knead in additional flour. Form a ball, oil, place in a bowl, cover and let rise in a warm place for 1½ hours or until doubled. Punch down.

Form into Christmas or Hanukkah characters, bread men or women, lions, elephants or menorahs. Decorate with raisins and almonds. Place on oiled baking sheets, cover and let rise in a warm place for another hour until doubled.

Preheat oven to 325 degrees. Brush with egg and apple juice concentrate mixture. Bake for 25 minutes until golden brown. Use in Christmas stockings or as prizes when playing dreidels.

Approximately 225 calories per serving
Over 35 grams carbohydrate per serving

SWEET DOUGH FIGURES

Makes 1 dozen

DOUGH INGREDIENTS

1 tablespoon baking yeast
1 cup warm pineapple juice
2 tablespoons oil
4 tablespoons frozen apple
  juice concentrate, thawed
1 teaspoon cinnamon
2¼ cups whole wheat pastry
  flour
¾ cup soy flour
¾ cup gluten flour

ICING INGREDIENTS

¼ cup soft butter
1½ cups non-instant milk powder
½ cup pineapple juice
1 teaspoon vanilla

DECORATING INGREDIENTS

Nuts
Raisins
Dried fruit

Preparation and Rising Time: 3 hours
Baking Time: 25 minutes

In a large bowl, sprinkle yeast over warm pineapple juice. Let stand 10 minutes until dissolved. Stir in oil and apple juice concentrate. In a separate bowl, mix cinnamon, pastry flour, soy flour and gluten flour. Beat 1½ cups of flour into liquids. Cover and allow to rise for 20 minutes to form a sponge. Beat in remaining flour mixture. Knead dough for 10 minutes until smooth and elastic. If dough becomes sticky, knead in additional flour. Form a ball, oil, place in a bowl, cover, set in a warm place and let rise for 1 hour or until doubled in bulk. Punch down and shape into Christmas figures, elves, Santa Clauses or Christmas trees, or Hanukkah figures, elephants or lions.

Place on oiled baking sheets, cover and let rise in a warm place until doubled. Preheat oven to 325 degrees. Bake for 25 minutes until golden brown. Cool on racks.

To make icing, mix butter, milk powder, pineapple juice and vanilla in an electric blender or food processor until smooth and thick. Frost entire figures or parts of figures and decorate with fruit and nuts. These figures can be used as stocking stuffers or as prizes for dreidels.

Approximately 225 calories per serving
Over 35 grams carbohydrate per serving

CHRISTMAS CANES
Makes 2 dozen

LIGHT DOUGH INGREDIENTS

1 cup whole wheat pastry flour
½ cup chestnut flour
½ teaspoon baking powder
2 tablespoons frozen apple
   juice concentrate, thawed
1 teaspoon peppermint extract
3 tablespoons oil
¼ cup apple juice

PINK DOUGH INGREDIENTS

1 cup whole wheat pastry flour
½ cup chestnut flour
½ teaspoon baking powder
2 tablespoons frozen apple
   juice concentrate, thawed
1 teaspoon peppermint extract
3 tablespoons oil
¼ cup beet juice
1 egg beaten with 1 tablespoon
   frozen apple juice concentrate, thawed

Preparation Time: 55 minutes
Baking Time: 10 to 15 minutes

To make light dough, mix pastry flour, chestnut flour and baking powder in a bowl, using a wire whisk. In a separate bowl, combine apple juice concentrate, peppermint extract, oil and apple juice. Gradually mix dry mixture into liquids to form a moldable dough. If dough is too dry, add juice; if too sticky, add flour. Chill for 30 minutes.

To make pink dough, combine pastry flour, chestnut flour and baking powder. In a separate bowl, mix apple juice concentrate, peppermint extract, oil and beet juice. Gradually mix dry ingredients into liquids to form a moldable dough. If dough is sticky, add more flour; if crumbly, add more liquid. Chill for 30 minutes

Shape teaspoon-size portions of each dough into thin rope by rolling on a lightly floured board. Twist ropes together and shape into canes. Place on oiled baking sheets.

Preheat oven to 350 degrees. Brush canes with egg-and-juice-concentrate mixture and bake for 10 to 15 minutes until done. These canes can be used as Christmas treats or as tree decorations.

Under 150 calories per serving
Approximately 20 grams carbohydrate per serving

MILK BALL ANGELS
Makes 6

¼ cup soft butter
1 cup non-instant skim milk
  powder
⅔ cup unsweetened shredded
  coconut
¼ cup apple or pineapple juice

In a bowl, cream butter, milk powder, coconut and juice to form a moldable dough. If dough is sticky, add more milk powder; if it is dry, add more juice. Press dough into an oiled cookie angel mold (available at kitchen specialty stores). Unmold and repeat until mixture is used. Cover with wax paper and refrigerate for 24 hours until confections have hardened.

Preparation Time: 25 minutes
Chilling Time: 24 hours

Approximately 225 calories per serving
Approximately 20 grams carbohydrate per serving

CUTOUT GINGER COOKIES
Makes 5 dozen

¼ cup blackstrap molasses
¼ cup frozen apple juice concentrate, thawed
½ cup oil

1 teaspoon ground ginger
1 teaspoon cinnamon
¼ teaspoon ground cloves
¼ teaspoon ground nutmeg
¼ teaspoon allspice
1 cup non-instant milk powder
4½ cups whole wheat pastry
  flour

In a bowl, mix molasses, apple juice concentrate and oil. In a separate bowl, mix ginger, cinnamon, cloves, nutmeg, allspice, milk powder and pastry flour with a wire whisk. Gradually mix dry ingredients into liquids to form a soft dough. If dough is sticky, add more flour; if crumbly, add more liquid. Cover and refrigerate for 1 hour. Roll dough ⅛-inch thick and cut with holiday cookie cutters. Place on oiled baking sheets.

Preheat oven to 375 degrees. Bake for 6 to 8 minutes until done. Cool on racks. These cookies may be seasoned for 2 weeks or served directly.

They can be used as stocking stuffers or as prizes when playing dreidels.

Preparation Time: 10 minutes
Chilling Time: 1 hour
Cutting Time: 20 minutes
Baking Time: 6 to 8 minutes

Approximately 150 calories per serving
Approximately 30 grams carbohydrate per serving

4

Natural Treats for the New Year

SNOW APPLES

6 McIntosh apples
⅓ cup pineapple juice
1 envelope unflavored gelatin
¼ cup water
3 egg whites
½ teaspoon vanilla
12 lemon leaves for garnish

Cut apples ½ inch from stem end. Dip cut surfaces in pineapple juice to avoid discoloring. Scoop out cut apples, leaving ⅛-inch shell. Discard top and core. Brush insides of shell with pineapple juice, wrap in plastic and refrigerate.

In a saucepan, combine juice and apple pulp. Cook over medium heat until apple pulp is tender. In a cup, dissolve gelatin in water. Remove apple pulp from heat and stir in gelatin mixture. Blend in an electric blender or food processor until smooth. Refrigerate until mixture mounds but is not fully set, about 2 hours.

Beat egg whites until stiff. Fold whites and vanilla into gelatin mixture. Spoon into apple shells and refrigerate until set. Arrange lemon leaves on a platter and top with snow apples to serve.

Preparation and Cooking Time:
3½ hours

Under 150 calories per serving
Under 30 grams carbohydrate per serving

SWEDISH FRUIT SOUP

Makes 10 6-ounce servings

¼ cup tapioca
2 cups mixed dried fruit
4 cups water
1 orange, unpeeled, halved and
    sliced
1 teaspoon cinnamon

*Preparation and Cooking Time: 2
hours*

In a saucepan, combine all ingredients. Cook covered over medium-low heat for 2 hours, stirring occasionally. Serve from a soup caldron while hot.

Under 150 calories per serving
Approximately 30 grams carbohydrate per serving

CHEESE-STUFFED PEARS

Serves 4

1 cup part-skim milk ricotta
    cheese
1 tablespoon milk
¼ teaspoon almond extract
½ cup slivered almonds
2 pears, halved and cored

Preparation Time: 15 minutes

With an electric mixer or food processor, beat cheese, milk and almond extract. Reserve 2 tablespoons slivered almonds and stir the remainder into cheese mixture. Place an ice cream scoop of mixture into each pear half and sprinkle with reserved almonds.

Under 150 calories per serving
Approximately 20 grams carbohydrate per serving

WHOLE SCARLET PEARS

Serves 6

¼ cup water
¼ cup pineapple juice
6 pears
10 ounces frozen unsweetened
    strawberries, thawed

Mix water and pineapple juice. Peel pears, leaving stem attached. Brush pears with pineapple juice and water. Place pears in a 2-quart casserole and pour in remaining pineapple juice mixture. Bake at 350 degrees for 50 minutes until pears are easily pierced with a fork. Remove from oven. Pour off water.

1 tablespoon frozen apple juice
concentrate, thawed

Sieve thawed strawberries and discard pulp. Stir in apple juice concentrate to form syrup. Pour over pears and allow to cool 30 minutes. Refrigerate for at least 12 hours, basting occasionally with strawberry syrup to color pears.

Seve individually on plates with knives and forks for eating.

Baking Time: 50 minutes
Marinating Time: 12 hours

Under 150 calories per serving
Approximately 30 grams carbohydrate per serving

WINTER FRUIT COMPOTE IN WINE SAUCE   *Serves 6 to 8*

3 cups red wine
1 cup mixed dried fruit
½ cup prunes, pitted
½ cup dried figs
2 apples, unpeeled and cored,
in wedges
2 pears, unpeeled and cored, in
wedges
1 3-inch stick cinnamon
1 lime, in wedges

In a bowl, combine wine, dried fruit, prunes and figs. Allow to stand overnight or for 8 hours until dried fruits are tender. Place in a pot with apples, pears, cinnamon stick and lime. Cook over medium-low heat, stirring occasionally, for 1 hour until apples and pears are tender.

Serve warm in individual dishes or from a soup caldron.

Marinating Time: 8 hours
Cooking Time: 1 hour

Over 225 calories per serving
Over 30 grams carbohydrate per serving

FANCY BAKED BANANAS WITH ALMOND SAUCE   *Serves 6*

3 firm bananas
1 teaspoon lemon juice
1 teaspoon melted butter
¼ teaspoon almond extract

1 cup water
1 tablespoon almond butter
1 tablespoon frozen apple juice
   concentrate, thawed
1 tablespoon arrowroot starch
   dissolved in 1 tablespoon
   water

*Preparation and Baking Time: 30
minutes*

Preheat oven to 375 degrees. Peel bananas and cut in half lengthwise. Brush with lemon juice, then with melted butter, and sprinkle with almond extract. Place in a shallow baking dish and bake for 20 minutes

While baking, prepare sauce. In an electric blender or food processor, blend water, almond butter and apple juice concentrate until smooth. Pour into a saucepan and heat until nearly boiling. Stir in arrowroot paste. Continue stirring for 3 minutes until sauce thickens to a glaze consistency.

Place baked bananas on platter and top with sauce while still warm.

Under 150 calories per serving
Under 30 grams carbohydrate per serving

CRANBERRY BANANA CREAM DELIGHT   *Serves 8 to 10*

Crumble Crust recipe (see p.
   17)
½ cup fresh cranberries
1 cup apple juice
2 tablespoons frozen apple
   juice concentrate, thawed
1 tablespoon cornstarch

1 banana, diced
1 teaspoon lemon juice
2 cups heavy cream

Prepare crumble mixture. Press half of mixture into a 9-inch pie plate and reserve the rest. In a saucepan, combine cranberries, apple juice, apple juice concentrate and cornstarch. Heat, stirring constantly, until thickened. Set aside to cool.

Toss diced banana in lemon juice to prevent discoloring. Whip cream. Gently fold cooled cranberry sauce and bananas into whipped cream to create a ripple effect. Spoon half of mixture into lined pie plate. Sprinkle with half of the remaining crumble crust. Spoon in the remaining whipped cream mixture and sprinkle with the rest of the crust combination. Chill for 2 hours before serving

Preparation Time: 20 minutes
Chilling Time: 2 hours

Over 250 calories per serving
Under 20 grams carbohydrate per serving

APPLESAUCE MOUSSE

Serves 6 to 8

1 envelope unflavored gelatin
¼ cup apple juice
2 cups unsweetened applesauce
1 cup milk
1 teaspoon cinnamon
2 tablespoons arrowroot starch

1 teaspoon grated orange peel
4 egg whites
2 apples, cored, cut in half and sliced thin, dipped in lemon juice

Dissolve gelatin in apple juice and set aside. In a saucepan, heat applesauce, milk, cinnamon and starch until thickened. While still hot, stir in gelatin and apple juice. Refrigerate for 1 hour until cold but not fully set. Add orange peel to egg whites and beat until stiff but not dry. Fold into chilled applesauce mixture. Pour into a 6-cup gelatin mold and chill until set, about 6 hours. Unmold and serve surrounded by apple slices.

Preparation Time: 15 minutes
Chilling Time: 6 hours

Under 150 calories per serving
Under 20 grams carbohydrate per serving

SHERRY APPLE MOUSSE

Serves 6 to 8

1 envelope unflavored gelatin
¼ cup frozen apple juice concentrate, thawed
2 cups unsweetened applesauce
3 eggs, separated
¼ cup cream sherry

Dissolve gelatin in apple juice concentrate, and set aside. In a saucepan, combine applesauce, egg yolks, sherry, cinnamon and orange peel. Bring to a gentle boil while stirring constantly. Remove from heat and stir in gelatin mixture. Refrigerate until cold but not set, approximately 30 minutes.

½ teaspoon cinnamon
½ teaspoon grated orange peel
1½ cups part-skim milk ricotta
cheese
2 apples cut in half, cored,
sliced thinly, dipped in
lemon juice

Preparation Time: 20 minutes
Chilling Time: 5 hours

Beat egg whites until stiff. Fold into applesauce mixture. Blend ricotta in an electric blender and fold in as well. Pour into a 6-cup gelatin mold and chill for 4 hours before serving. Unmold and serve surrounded by apple slices.

Under 150 calories per serving
Approximately 30 grams carbohydrate per serving

CREAMY APPLE WALNUT CHEESECAKE   *Serves 10 to 12*

Crumble Crust recipe (see p. 17)
3 eggs, separated
1 tablespoon grated lemon peel
½ cup frozen apple juice concentrate, thawed
1 teaspoon vanilla
2 8-ounce packages cream
cheese
2 tablespoons soy flour
1 cup heavy cream, whipped
10 walnut halves

Prepare crumble crust according to instructions. Press mixture into a 9-inch springform pan and refrigerate. Preheat oven to 350 degrees.

Beat egg yolks until lemon-colored. Add lemon peel and gradually mix in apple juice concentrate and vanilla. Stir in cream cheese and flour until smooth mixture is formed.

Beat egg whites until stiff but not dry. Fold into cream cheese mixture. Fold in whipped cream. Pour into chilled springform pan lined with refrigerated crust. Bake for 50 minutes until set. Turn off oven and allow cake to remain until oven has fully cooled. Place walnut halves evenly around edge of cake and refrigerate for at least 1 hour. Before serving loosen edges with knife and remove from springform pan.

Preparation Time: 15 minutes
Baking Time: 50 minutes

Over 250 calories per serving
Approximately 20 grams carbohydrate per serving

SWEDISH ALMOND TARTS

Serves 12

1 cup whole wheat pastry flour
1 cup whole wheat flour
⅓ cup safflower oil or soft butter
5–6 tablespoons ice water
6 egg whites
½ teaspoon almond extract
¾ cup ground almonds
12 teaspoons unsweetened raspberry or strawberry preserves

Combine flours. Stir in oil or butter with a fork until mixture resembles coarse meal. Stir in ice water until dough forms a ball. Divide dough into 12 balls and refrigerate for 30 minutes. Place a well-oiled 5-inch square of heavy duty aluminum foil under each ball and place a 5-inch square piece of wax paper over each. Flatten with rolling pin into 5-inch circles. Remove wax paper. With pastry scissors, trim dough and foil into perfect circles. Shape foil and pastry together, turning up edge 1½ inches in a decorative manner. Preheat oven to 375 degrees.

Beat egg whites and almond extract until stiff peaks form. Fold in almonds. Spread 1 teaspoon preserves over each tart. Cover with egg and almond filling and bake for 25 minutes until shells are lightly browned and meringue is lightly browned. Cool and remove foil before serving.

Preparation Time: 50 minutes
Baking Time: 25 minutes

Under 150 calories per serving
Approximately 25 grams carbohydrate per serving

CAROB CHEESECAKE

Serves 12

Crumble Crust recipe (see p. 17)
2 cups part-skim milk ricotta cheese
1½ cups 2% cottage cheese
3 eggs, separated
1 cup apple juice
2 teaspoons vanilla

Preheat oven to 350 degrees. Line 10-inch springform pan with crumble crust mixture. Bake for 10 minutes and remove from oven.

In a blender or food processor, blend ricotta, cottage cheese, egg yolks, apple juice, vanilla and carob powder until smooth. Pour into partially baked crust and bake for 50 minutes until top is slightly cracked and a knife inserted comes out clean.

¾ cup roasted carob powder

1 cup sour cream

½ cup roasted carob powder

2 tablespoons frozen apple
juice concentrate, thawed

Preparation Time: 15 minutes
Baking Time: 1 hour

Combine sour cream, carob powder and apple juice concentrate. Spread over cheesecake and cool completely before serving.

Approximately 250 calories per serving
Under 30 grams carbohydrate per serving

APPLE TURNOVERS WITH CARDAMOM SAUCE
Serves 18

Flaky Pastry Dough recipe (see p. 16)

5 apples, unpeeled and grated

1 tablespoon frozen apple juice
concentrate, thawed

3 tablespoons cornstarch

2 cups apple juice

2 tablespoons apple butter

1½ teaspoons ground cardamom

2 tablespoons arrowroot starch
mixed with 1 tablespoon
water

Preparation Time: 50 minutes
Baking Time: 20 minutes

Preheat oven to 425 degrees. Roll chilled dough into a 12 x 24-inch rectangle on a lightly floured board. Cut into 18 4-inch squares. In a bowl, mix grated apple, apple juice concentrate and starch. Place approximately 2 tablespoons apple mixure on each square. Fold squares to form triangles, and seal edges with prongs of a fork. Bake for 20 minutes until golden brown.

While turnovers bake, prepare sauce. Heat apple juice, apple butter and cardamom nearly to boiling. Stir in starch paste. Continue stirring 3 minutes until thickened. Serve hot turnovers with warm sauce in a creamer or gravy boat.

Under 150 calories per serving
Under 30 grams carbohydrate per serving

APPLE PRUNE STRUDEL

Serves 24 to 28

Strudel recipe (see p. 17)
6 cups unpeeled, grated apples
2 cups pitted prunes, chopped
¼ cup orange juice
2 tablespoons orange peel
2 teaspoons cinnamon
⅓ cup cornstarch

Preparation Time: 1 hour
Baking Time: 40 minutes

Prepare strudel dough according to instructions, and roll thin. In a bowl, mix apples, prunes, orange juice, orange peel, cinnamon and cornstarch. Place on dough and roll strudel according to recipe directions. Bake at 450 degrees for 10 minutes, reduce heat and bake at 400 degrees for 20 minutes until lightly browned and crisp.

Approximately 225 calories per serving
Under 30 grams carbohydrate per serving

SESAME RICE RING

Serves 15

1½ cups sweet brown rice
4 cups water
2 cups apple cider
2 teaspoons vanilla
¼ cup tahini
¼ cup apple butter
3 envelopes unflavored gelatin
    dissolved in ½ cup apple
    juice

Preparation Time: 2 hours
Chilling Time: 3 hours

Combine rice and water in a covered pan. Bring to a boil, reduce heat and cook for 1 hour. Add apple cider and cook for 45 minutes until soft and creamy. Remove from heat and stir in vanilla, tahini, apple butter and dissolved gelatin. Pour into a 2-quart gelatin mold and chill until set. Remove from mold to serve.

Under 150 calories per serving
Approximately 30 grams carbohydrate per serving

GERMAN CAROB TORTE

Serves 10 to 12

CAKE INGREDIENTS

½ cup safflower oil
1¼ cups apple juice
¼ cup liquid barley malt
1¼ cups whole wheat pastry
    flour
1¼ cups brown rice flour
⅓ cup roasted carob powder
¼ cup non-instant milk powder
4 teaspoons baking powder
2 teaspoons almond extract
4 egg whites

FILLING INGREDIENTS

3 tablespoons brown rice flour
4 egg yolks
½ cup water
1 cup pineapple juice
2 cups unsweetened shredded
    coconut
2 cups chopped walnuts
1 teaspoon almond extract

Preparation Time: 20 minutes
Baking Time: 1 hour

Preheat oven to 350 degrees. In a bowl, combine oil, apple juice and liquid barley malt. In a separate bowl, mix whole wheat pastry flour, brown rice flour, carob powder, milk powder and baking powder. Stir into liquid combination. Form a smooth batter. Stir in almond extract. Beat egg whites until stiff. Fold into batter. Pour into 2 well-oiled 9-inch cake pans. Bake for 1 hour or until a toothpick inserted into the center of the cake comes out clean. Remove from pans and cool on racks.

To prepare filling, combine rice flour, egg yolks, water and pineapple juice in a saucepan. Cook over medium heat, stirring constantly, for 5 minutes until mixture thickens. Stir in coconut, walnuts and almond extract. Allow to cool.

To assemble cake, cut each layer in half to form four layers. Spread filling between each layer and frost with remaining filling.

Approximately 225 calories per serving
Over 35 grams carbohydrate per serving

NEW YEAR'S APPLE GINGER PUDDING

Serves 15

1½ cups whole wheat pastry
  flour
1½ cups brown rice flour
2 teaspoons baking soda
1 teaspoon cinnamon
½ teaspoon allspice
½ teaspoon ground cardamom
½ teaspoon nutmeg
½ cup safflower oil or melted
  butter
2 eggs
¼ cup blackstrap molasses
4 teaspoons grated fresh ginger
  root
1 cup unsweetened applesauce
⅔ cup hot apple juice
½ cup raisins

Mix dry ingredients in a large bowl. In a separate bowl, combine oil or melted butter, eggs, molasses, ginger root, applesauce, apple juice and raisins. Gradually stir liquid mixture into dry ingredients to form a smooth batter. Pour into a lightly oiled 6-cup metal mold. Place a rack in a Dutch oven or covered roasting pan. Pour in water to the level of the rack. Bring water to a boil. Place a double thickness of aluminum foil over mold, secure with a string or elastic band and place covered mold on rack, then cover Dutch oven. Continue to boil for 3 to 4 hours until pudding is firm and a knife inserted into the center comes out clean. (If water evaporates, add more as needed.)

When cooked and cooled, this pudding can be gift-wrapped in colored foil or placed in a festive tin box as a hostess gift.

Preparation Time: 10 minutes
Cooking Time: 3 to 4 hours

Approximately 225 calories per serving
Over 40 grams carbohydrate per serving

CAROB PEANUT WAFERS

Serves 48

12 slices whole wheat bread
½ cup peanut butter
4 tablespoons safflower oil
2 tablespoons carob powder
1 tablespoon frozen apple juice
  concentrate, thawed

Remove crusts from bread to form a neat square. Save crusts and cut bread into 4 strips. Place crusts and strips on a dry baking sheet and bake at 150 degrees for 2 to 3 hours until crisp. Place crusts in a blender or food processor and blend to fine dry crumbs. Place crumbs on a plate. On a separate plate, mix peanut butter, oil, carob powder and apple juice concentrate. Spread mixture on each dry strip of bread and cover completely. Roll in breadcrumbs and return to 150-degree oven for 15 minutes or until coating is dry.

These wafers make a lovely holiday gift when arranged in a decorative cookie tin.

Preparation Time: 20 minutes
Baking Time 3–4 hours

Under 150 calories per serving
Under 20 grams carbohydrate per serving

BUTTERY SNOWBALLS

Serves 24

1 cup non-instant skim milk
   powder
½ cup soft unsalted butter
1 teaspoon cardamom
1 teaspoon vanilla
3–4 tablespoons frozen apple
   juice concentrate, thawed
¾ cup unsweetened shredded
   coconut

Preparation Time: 10 minutes

Cream together milk powder, butter, cardamom, vanilla and apple juice concentrate. If dough is sticky, add more milk powder; if too dry, add water. Form into balls and roll in coconut. Cover with plastic or wax paper and refrigerate for 24 hours until firm.

These simple confections make a nice hostess gift when placed in a glass canister and tied with a bow.

Under 150 calories per serving
Under 20 grams carbohydrate per serving

5

Healthy Hearts, Candies and Cakes for Valentine's Day

STRUFOLI

2½ cups whole wheat pastry
  flour
2 tablespoons gluten flour
4 eggs, beaten
1 egg yolk
2 tablespoons soft butter
1 tablespoon grated lemon peel
1 teaspoon lemon juice
1 tablespoon frozen apple juice
  concentrate, thawed
Safflower oil for frying
½ cup liquid barley malt
½ cup water

Preparation Time: 10 minutes
Frying Time: 20 minutes
Assembling Time: 10 minutes

In a bowl, combine pastry flour and gluten flour. Make a well in flour and add eggs, egg yolk, butter, lemon peel, lemon juice and apple juice concentrate. Stir with a wooden spoon to form a soft dough. Turn onto a lightly floured board and knead just until smooth. If dough is sticky, add just enough flour to eliminate sticking.

Pull off ¼-cup-size pieces of dough and roll into ropes ½ inch in diameter. Cut into ¼-inch slices. Heat oil to 375 degrees and drop in small pieces of dough. Fry until lightly browned and remove from oil. Drain on paper towels.

In a saucepan, heat malt and water to boiling. Boil for 5 minutes. Arrange fried balls of dough in a mound on a serving plate and pour hot malt mixture over strufoli.

Approximately 225 calories per serving
Over 35 grams carbohydrate per serving

CAROB FONDUE

1½ cups roasted carob powder
1½ cups water
1 tablespoon cornstarch
2 tablespoons butter
1 cup whole frozen unsweetened strawberries
2 bananas, sliced
2 apples, sliced
1 tablespoon pineapple juice
2 oranges, peeled and in
  wedges

Preparation and Cooking Time:
10 minutes

In a saucepan, combine carob powder, water, cornstarch and butter. Heat, stirring occasionally, for 5 minutes until mixture thickens. Pour into a fondue pot to keep warm. Arrange strawberries in the center of a serving dish. Toss bananas and apples with pineapple juice to prevent discoloring. Arrange on a plate along with orange wedges. Serve as dippers for carob fondue.

Under 150 calories per serving
Under 30 grams carbohydrate per serving

STRAWBERRY PROFITEROLES *with Carob Sauce*

Cream Puff Pastry recipe (see
  p. 19)
2 cups frozen unsweetened
  strawberries, thawed
1 envelope unflavored gelatin
1¼ cups part-skim milk ricotta
  cheese
1 teaspoon vanilla

½ cup roasted carob powder
¾ cup water
1 tablespoon cornstarch

Preheat oven to 425 degrees. Prepare cream puff pastry and drop dough by teaspoonfuls on a cookie sheet sprayed with non-stick vegetable cooking spray. Bake for 25 minutes until lightly browned. Turn off oven and leave profiteroles in oven until cooled.

Drain strawberries. Place juice in a saucepan and sprinkle with gelatin. Heat over low heat until dissolved. Remove from heat. Place gelatin mixture, strawberries, ricotta and vanilla in an electric blender or food processor and blend until smooth. Chill for 3 hours until softly set.

With a sharp knife cut a slit in each profiterole. Spoon 1 tablespoon filling in each opening. Refrigerate until sauce is made.

In a saucepan, combine carob powder, water and cornstarch. Cook, stirring occasionally, for 5 minutes, until sauce thickens. Arrange profiteroles on a plate and pour sauce over them just before serving.

Preparation Time: 30 minutes
Chilling Time: 3 hours
Baking Time: 25 minutes
Assembling Time: 20 minutes

Under 150 calories per serving
Under 20 grams carbohydrate per serving

BLACK FOREST CAKE

Serves 12 to 16

1 12-ounce package frozen unsweetened dark cherries
½ cup sweet red wine
½ cup safflower oil
5 eggs, separated
⅓ cup liquid barley malt
1 cup apple juice
1¼ cups whole wheat pastry
flour
1 cup brown rice flour
¾ cup roasted carob powder
4 teaspoons baking powder

1 stick soft unsalted butter
2 cups heavy cream
1½ teaspoons vanilla
1 Burry's Health Food Carob
Bar

Place cherries in a bowl to thaw and cover with wine. Preheat oven to 350 degrees. In a separate bowl, beat oil, egg yolks, malt and apple juice. In another bowl, combine pastry flour, brown rice flour, carob powder and baking powder. Mix well with a wire whisk. Gradually mix dry combination into liquid ingredients to form a smooth batter. Beat egg whites until stiff and fold into batter. Pour into an oiled 10-inch springform pan. Bake for 90 minutes until a toothpick comes out clean when inserted. Remove from oven and cool on a rack while preparing fillings.

Drain cherries. Mix 2 tablespoons drained-off wine juice with butter until smooth. Whip cream and vanilla.

When cake is completely cooled, cut it into three thin layers. Spread the first layer with one-quarter of the butter-and-wine mixture, then one-quarter of whipped cream. Press one-half of drained cherries into whipped cream and distribute evenly over the top of the layer. Spread bottom of second layer with one-quarter of butter-and-wine mixture and place it over the first layer. Spread one-quarter of the butter, one-quarter of the whipped cream and the rest of the cherries on the top of the second layer. Cover with third layer. Frost with remaining whipped cream. Shave carob bar with a vegetable peeler to form curls of carob and cover with curls. Refrigerate until ready to serve.

Preparation Time: 15 minutes
Baking Time: 90 minutes
Assembling Time: 20 minutes

Over 250 calories per serving
Over 35 grams carbohydrate per serving

CAROB STRAWBERRY CHEESE ROLL
Serves 12

CAKE INGREDIENTS
1 cup whole wheat pastry flour
1 cup brown rice flour
1 cup roasted carob powder
2 teaspoons baking powder
6 eggs, separated
1⅓ cups apple juice
⅓ cup liquid barley malt
1 teaspoon vanilla

1 cup unsweetened shredded coconut

FILLING INGREDIENTS
1 envelope unflavored gelatin
½ cup apple juice
1½ cups frozen unsweetened strawberries, thawed
2 tablespoons frozen apple juice concentrate, thawed
1 cup part-skim milk ricotta cheese

Preheat oven to 375 degrees. In a bowl, mix pastry flour, brown rice flour, carob powder and baking powder with a wire whisk until evenly distributed. In a separate bowl, beat egg yolks, apple juice, malt and vanilla. Gradually stir liquids into flour combination to form a smooth batter. Beat egg whites until stiff. Fold into batter. Oil a 15 x 10 x 1-inch jelly roll pan, line with wax paper and grease wax paper. Pour batter into prepared pan. Bake for 15 minutes or until a toothpick comes out clean when inserted into the center. While cake is baking, place coconut in an electric blender or food processor and blend to a fine powder. Sprinkle coconut powder over a clean dry kitchen towel. Remove cake from oven, turn onto prepared towel, peel off wax paper, cut off hard edges for easy rolling, and roll in towel. Allow to cool completely while rolled.

To make filling, sprinkle gelatin over apple juice in a saucepan. Heat over low heat until gelatin has dissolved. Place gelatin mixture, strawberries, apple juice concentrate and ricotta in an electric blender or food processor and blend until smooth. Chill mixture until softly set, about 2 hours.

FROSTING
¼ cup soft unsalted butter
½ cup non-instant skim milk powder
¼ cup roasted carob powder
½ cup apple juice
½ Burry's Health Food Carob Bar

Preparation Time: 15 minutes
Chilling Time: 2 hours
Baking Time: 15 minutes
Assembling Time: 15 minutes

Unroll cake carefully and spread with filling. To start rerolling, lift end of towel. Place roll seam side down on a serving plate. To make frosting, blend butter, milk powder, carob powder and apple juice in an electric blender or food processor. Frost roll. Using a vegetable peeler, shave carob bar to make carob curls. Garnish roll with curls. Serve immediately or refrigerate until serving time.

Approximately 225 calories per serving
Over 35 grams carbohydrate per serving

VALENTINE'S CAROB CAKE — *Serves 12*

CAKE INGREDIENTS
½ cup safflower oil
5 eggs, separated
1 cup plain yogurt
½ cup liquid barley malt ·
¾ cup whole wheat pastry flour
¾ cup brown rice flour
1½ cups roasted carob powder
3 teaspoons baking powder

FROSTING INGREDIENTS
2 tablespoons butter
¾ cup roasted carob powder
½ cup water

Preheat oven to 350 degrees. To make cake, combine oil, egg yolks, yogurt and liquid barley malt in a bowl. In a separate bowl, stir pastry flour, brown rice flour, carob powder and baking powder with a wire whisk. Gradually add liquid ingredients to dry ingredients to form a smooth batter. Beat egg whites until stiff and fold into batter. Pour into a well-oiled heart-shaped baking tin. Bake for 90 minutes or until a toothpick comes out clean when inserted into the center of the cake. Remove cake from tin and cool on a wire rack.

To make carob frosting, combine butter, carob powder and water in an electric blender or food processor. When cake is cool, pour frosting over cake and let it drip over sides.

DECORATING FROSTING
INGREDIENTS

2 tablespoons soft butter
¼ cup apple juice
¾ cup milk powder
1 teaspoon vanilla

Preparation Time: 15 minutes
Baking Time: 90 minutes

To make decorating frosting, blend butter, apple juice, milk powder and vanilla in an electric blender or food processor until smooth and thick. Place frosting in a decorator bag and decorate cake as desired.

Approximately 225 calories per serving
Over 35 grams carbohydrate per serving

REFRIGERATOR CAROB CHEESECAKE

Serves 12

Crumble Crust recipe (see p. 17)
2 envelopes unflavored gelatin
½ cup apple juice
1 cup roasted carob powder
1 cup water
1 tablespoon cornstarch
2½ cups 1% cottage cheese
3 egg whites
2 tablespoons grated Burry's Health Food Carob Bar

Preparation Time: 20 minutes
Chilling Time: 3 hours

Line a 10-inch springform pan with crumble pie crust. Refrigerate for 15 minutes while preparing filling. Sprinkle gelatin over apple juice.

In a saucepan, combine 1 cup carob powder, water and cornstarch. Cook over medium heat, stirring occasionally, until thickened. Stir in gelatin mixture and remove from heat. Place in an electric blender along with cottage cheese and blend until smooth. Beat egg whites until stiff. Fold into carob cheese mixture and pour into chilled crumble crust. Chill for 3 hours until firm and sprinkle with grated carob bar.

Under 150 calories per serving
Under 20 grams carbohydrate per serving

CAROB CHIFFON PIE

Serves 8

½ Flaky or Stretchy Pastry
  Dough recipe (see p. 16)
2 envelopes unflavored gelatin
⅓ cup apple juice
¾ cup roasted carob powder
½ cup water
1 teaspoon vanilla
5 eggs, separated
¾ cup heavy cream
2 tablespoons grated Burry's
  Health Food Carob Bar

Preheat oven to 400 degrees. Prepare pie dough and line a 9-inch pie plate. Bake for 20 minutes until lightly browned. Remove from oven to cool.

Sprinkle gelatin over apple juice to dissolve. In a saucepan, combine carob powder, water, vanilla and egg yolks. Cook over medium heat without boiling, stirring occasionally, for 10 minutes until thickened. Stir in gelatin mixture and remove from heat. Chill for 1 hour until mixture thickens to the consistency of custard but is not set.

Beat egg whites until stiff and fold into gelatin mixture. Whip cream and fold in. Pour into baked pie shell and refrigerate for 2 hours until set. Sprinkle with grated carob bar.

Preparation Time: 30 minutes
Chilling Time: 3 hours

Approximately 225 calories per serving
Approximately 20 grams carbohydrate per serving

STRAWBERRY CHIFFON PIE

Serves 8

½ Flaky Pie Crust recipe (see
  p. 16)
2 envelopes unflavored gelatin
½ cup apple juice
¾ cup milk
3 tablespoons cornstarch or 5
  egg yolks
1 tablespoon frozen apple juice
  concentrate, thawed
5 egg whites

Preheat oven to 400 degrees. Line pie plate with dough and bake for 20 minutes until lightly browned. Sprinkle gelatin over apple juice. In a saucepan, combine milk, cornstarch or egg yolks and apple juice concentrate. Cook over medium heat, stirring constantly, until thickened. Stir in gelatin mixture and 2 cups thawed strawberries. Chill for 1 hour until mixture is the consistency of custard but not set.

Remove from refrigerator, beat egg whites until stiff and fold into strawberry mixture. Pour into baked pie shell and chill 1 hour until set.

2 cups frozen unsweetened
  strawberries, thawed
1 cup apple juice
1 tablespoon cornstarch
½ cup frozen unsweetened
  strawberries, thawed

Preparation Time: 30 minutes
Chilling Time: 3 hours

In a saucepan, combine apple juice and cornstarch. Cook, stirring occasionally, until thickened. Stir in strawberries. Cool and serve with pie.

Under 150 calories per serving
Approximately 20 grams carbohydrate per serving

CAROB MOUSSE

Serves 12 to 16

2 envelopes unflavored gelatin
½ cup water
1½ cups roasted carob powder
4 tablespoons cornstarch or 6
  egg yolks
1½ cups water
6 egg whites
1 cup heavy cream, whipped
1 teaspoon vanilla
1 Burry's Health Food Carob
  Bar, grated

Preparation Time: 20 minutes
Chilling Time: 2 to 3 hours

Sprinkle gelatin over water. In a saucepan, combine carob powder, cornstarch or egg yolks and 1½ cups water. Cook over medium heat, stirring occasionally, until thickened. Stir in gelatin mixture and remove from heat. Chill for 1 hour until mixture is the consistency of custard but is not set.

Beat egg whites until stiff and fold into gelatin mixture. Fold in whipped cream and vanilla. Gently stir in grated carob. Pour into a 2-quart mold and chill for 2 hours until set. Unmold and serve.

Approximately 225 calories per serving
Approximately 20 grams carbohydrate per serving

STRAWBERRY CAROB PARFAITS
Serves 8

2 envelopes unflavored gelatin
½ cup apple juice
⅔ cup milk
3 tablespoons cornstarch or 5 egg yolks
2 cups frozen unsweetened strawberries, thawed
3 tablespoons frozen apple juice concentrate, thawed

5 egg whites

¾ cup roasted carob powder
½ cup water

Preparation Time: 20 minutes
Chilling Time: 3 hours

Sprinkle gelatin over apple juice. In a saucepan, combine milk and cornstarch or egg yolks. Heat over medium heat, stirring constantly until mixture thickens. Stir in gelatin mixture and remove from heat. Stir in strawberries and apple juice concentrate. Refrigerate for 1 hour until mixture is the texture of custard but is not set.

Beat egg whites until stiff and fold into chilled gelatin mixture. Spoon into parfait glasses and chill for 2 hours until set. In a saucepan, combine carob powder and water. Cook until thickened. Cool and spoon over strawberry parfaits just before serving.

Approximately 150 calories per serving
Approximately 20 grams carbohydrate per serving

VALENTINE'S STRAWBERRY TARTS
Serves 8

Stretchy Pie Dough recipe (see p. 16)
3 cups frozen unsweetened strawberries, thawed
3 tablespoons frozen apple juice concentrate, thawed
4 tablespoons arrowroot starch

Preparation Time: 25 minutes
Baking Time: 20 minutes

Preheat oven to 375 degrees. Divide dough into 8 parts. Place each part on a 5-inch square of heavy duty aluminum foil. Roll into a circle. Using pastry scissors, cut foil with dough attached into a heart shape. Make a tart by turning up a 1-inch flute.

In a bowl, combine strawberries, juice concentrate and starch. Spoon mixture into prepared tarts and bake for 20 minutes until lightly browned.

Approximately 150 calories per serving
Approximately 20 grams carbohydrate per serving

ITALIAN MERINGUES
Serves 6

MERINGUE INGREDIENTS
¼ cup liquid barley malt
¼ cup water
6 egg whites
¼ teaspoon cream of tartar
1 teaspoon almond extract

FILLING INGREDIENTS
¾ cup frozen unsweetened
  strawberries, thawed
2 tablespoons frozen apple
  juice concentrate, thawed
1 tablespoon cornstarch

Preheat oven to 200 degrees. To make meringues, combine malt and water in a saucepan and bring to a boil. Continue to boil for 15 minutes until mixture reaches soft-ball stage. While malt and water boil, beat egg whites until foamy and add cream of tartar and almond extract. Beat for 15 minutes until whites are stiff and glossy. Gradually add malt mixture while continuing to beat. Spray cookie sheet with a non-stick vegetable spray. With a spoon make 6 mounds of meringue on baking sheet. Shape indentations in the center to hold filling after baking. Bake for 1 to 2 hours until meringue is lightly browned and completely dried out. Remove from baking sheet with a spatula and cool on a rack.

To make filling, drain strawberries, reserving juice. Combine strawberry juice, apple juice concentrate and cornstarch in a saucepan. Cook over medium heat, stirring constantly, until mixture thickens. Stir in strawberries and remove from heat to cool. Spoon into meringue shells and serve immediately.

Preparation Time: 25 minutes
Baking Time: 1 to 2 hours

Approximately 150 calories per serving
Approximately 20 grams carbohydrate per serving

STRAWBERRY CRÊPES
Serves 8 to 10

Delicate Whole Wheat Crêpes
  or Low Calorie Eggless
  Crêpes recipe (see p. 18)
1 cup part-skim milk ricotta
  cheese

Prepare crêpes according to directions. In a blender or food processor, purée ricotta and apple juice concentrate until smooth. Drain strawberries, reserving juice. Stir drained berries into ricotta mixture. Roll 2 scant tablespoons of ricotta strawberry mixture into each crêpe.

1 tablespoon frozen apple juice
concentrate, thawed
2 cups frozen unsweetened
strawberries, thawed
½ cup apple juice
1 tablespoon cornstarch

In a saucepan, combine strawberry juice, apple juice and cornstarch. Cook, stirring constantly, until thickened. Pour over crêpes while hot.

Preparation Time: 10 minutes
Cooking Time: 30 minutes

Approximately 150 calories per serving
Approximately 20 grams carbohydrate per serving

LAYERED PEANUT BUTTER CAROB TOFFEE   *Makes 64 candies*

PEANUT BUTTER TOFFEE IN-
GREDIENTS
½ cup liquid barley malt
½ cup milk
1 tablespoon non-instant skim
milk powder
1 tablespoon soft peanut butter

CAROB TOFFEE INGREDIENTS
½ cup liquid barley malt
½ cup milk
2 tablespoons roasted carob
powder
1 tablespoon soft butter

Preparation and Cooking Time:
35 minutes
Cooling Time: 3 hours

In a saucepan, bring malt, milk and milk powder to a gentle boil. Allow to boil 15 minutes and stir in peanut butter. Remove from heat and pour into a well-oiled 8-inch square pan.

For carob layer, bring malt, milk and carob powder to a gentle boil. Continue to boil 15 minutes and stir in soft butter. Pour over peanut butter layer. While warm cut into 1-inch squares.

When cool, wrap in plastic wrap or with colored aluminum foil and place in a decorative candy box to be given as a Valentine's Day present. Candy will keep best if refrigerated until served.

Under 150 calories per candy
(Malt is a concentrated, high-carbohydrate food)

ALMOND CRUNCH

Makes 32 pieces of candy

2 tablespoons butter
½ cup liquid barley malt
1¼ cups almonds
1 teaspoon cinnamon

In a heavy frying pan, melt butter. Stir in malt and boil for 5 minutes until mixture reaches soft-ball stage. Stir in nuts and cinnamon. Pour into a well-oiled 8-inch square pan and spread evenly. While still warm, cut into 1 x 2-inch rectangles. When cool, break apart and place in a decorative candy box alone or with other candies as a Valentine's Day gift.

Preparation and Cooking Time:
10 minutes

Under 150 calories per candy
(Malt is a concentrated, high-carbohydrate food)

NUT-COATED CARAMELS

Makes 36 candies

¾ cup liquid barley malt
¼ cup non-instant skim milk
   powder
⅓ cup finely ground nuts

In a heavy pan, combine malt and milk powder. Heat, stirring constantly, until mixture boils gently for 3 minutes. Remove from heat and roll into six 6-inch ropes. Roll each rope in ground nuts to coat, and cut into six 1-inch candies.

   Placed in a candy box or candy jar, this makes a lovely gift.

Preparation and Cooking Time:
20 minutes

Under 150 calories per candy
(Malt is a concentrated, high-carbohydrate food)

CAROB CAPPED COCONUT CHEWS

Makes 36 candies

½ cup liquid barley malt
⅔ cup non-instant skim milk
  powder
½ cup unsweetened shredded
  coconut
2 tablespoons soft butter
¾ cup roasted carob powder
⅓ cup water
½ teaspoon vanilla

In a heavy pan, heat malt. Stir in milk powder and coconut. Remove from heat and form into 36 balls. Place on wax paper to cool.

In an electric blender or food processor blend butter, carob powder, water and vanilla until smooth and thick. If mixture is not thick enough, add more carob powder, 1 teaspoonful at a time. Dip candies in carob mixture to coat top. Allow to stand in cool air for 2 hours until carob coating sets.

Place in a decorative candy box to be given as a present or served as Valentine's Day treats.

*Preparation and Cooking Time:
30 minutes*

*Under 150 calories per candy
(Malt is a concentrated, high-carbohydrate food)*

MOLASSES COCONUT CHEWS

Makes 36 candies

2 tablespoons blackstrap molasses
¾ cup liquid barley malt
3 tablespoons non-instant skim
  milk powder
2 cups unsweetened shredded
  coconut

In a heavy pan, combine molasses, malt and milk powder. Boil, stirring constantly, for 5 minutes. Stir in coconut, remove from heat, and shape into balls with hands moistened with water.

Place in a candy dish tied with a bow or in a decorative candy box for a fine Valentine's Day gift.

*Preparation and Cooking Time:
10 minutes*

*Under 150 calories per candy
(Blackstrap molasses is a concentrated, high-carbohydrate food)*

CREAM CARAMELS

Makes 64 candies

1⅓ cups liquid barley malt
½ cup butter
2 cups light cream
3 tablespoons non-instant skim
  milk powder

In a heavy pan, combine malt, butter, cream and milk powder to a smooth mixture. Heat to a gentle boil. Continue to boil, stirring occasionally, until mixture reaches soft-ball stage. Pour into an 8-inch square pan oiled with safflower oil. While still warm cut into 1-inch square candies. When cooled, wrap individually in wax paper, twisting both ends.

Place in a candy jar or decorative candy box to serve at parties or to use as a Valentine's Day gift.

Preparation and Cooking Time:
20 minutes

Under 150 calories per candy
(Malt is a concentrated, high-carbohydrate food)

RAISIN SESAME CLUSTERS

Makes 36 candies

3 tablespoons blackstrap molasses
⅓ cup liquid barley malt
1 tablespoon roasted carob powder
1 cup sesame seeds
1 cup raisins

In a heavy pan, combine molasses, malt and carob powder. Heat mixture and boil for 3 minutes. Stir in sesame seeds and raisins until mixture is well distributed. Remove from heat and quickly drop by spoonfuls onto well-oiled wax paper.

When cool, place in a decorative candy box and give as a Valentine's Day gift.

Preparation and Cooking Time:
10 minutes

Under 150 calories per candy
(Malt is a concentrated, high-carbohydrate food)

CARAMEL PECAN CLUSTERS

Makes 40 candies

¾ cup liquid barley malt
¼ cup milk
½ cup non-instant milk powder
2 cups pecans

In a heavy pan, combine malt, milk and non-instant milk powder. Bring to a boil. Continue boiling, while stirring, for 5 minutes until mixture reaches soft-ball stage. Stir in pecans and drop mixture by spoonfuls onto a well-oiled sheet of wax paper.

When cool, place in a candy box or a dish decorated with a bow for a lovely Valentine's Day gift.

Preparation and Cooking Time:
10 minutes

Under 150 calories per candy
(Malt is a concentrated, high-carbohydrate food)

GLAZED WALNUTS

Makes 2 cups candy

¼ cup liquid barley malt
2 tablespoons water
1 teaspoon ground cardamom
2 teaspoons vanilla
1 tablespoon butter
2 cups walnuts

In a saucepan, combine malt, water and cardamom. Heat to a boil. Continue to boil until soft-ball stage is reached. Stir in vanilla, butter and walnuts. Turn onto a well-oiled sheet of wax paper. When nearly cooled, break walnuts apart.

When completely cooled and placed in a candy box or decorative candy jar, these candies make easy and festive Valentine's Day gifts.

Preparation and Cooking Time:
10 minutes

Under 150 calories per candy
(Malt is a concentrated, high-carbohydrate food)

MINT CAROB LOG

Makes 36 candies

½ cup soft unsalted butter
1 cup non-instant skim milk
  powder
1 tablespoon natural crème de
  menthe flavoring
2–3 tablespoons frozen apple
  juice concentrate, thawed
1 Burry's Health Food Carob
  Bar, finely grated

Preparation Time: 10 minutes
Chilling Time: 36 hours

Cream butter, milk powder, crème de menthe flavoring and apple juice concentrate, 1 tablespoon at a time to form a soft dough. Shape into 3 logs. Roll in grated carob. Wrap in wax paper and refrigerate for 12 hours. Slice logs into 36 thin candies. Place wax paper between slices and refrigerate for 24 hours until hard.

This candy makes a lovely Valentine's Day gift if placed in a decorative box or jar. It should be refrigerated until served.

Under 150 calories per candy
Under 20 grams carbohydrate per candy

PRALINES

Makes 12 candies

½ cup liquid barley malt
½ cup milk
1 tablespoon butter
1 cup chopped pecans

Preparation and Cooking Time:
15 minutes
Cooling Time: 30 minutes

Bring malt and milk to a boil. Stir in butter and continue to boil for 5 minutes or until mixture reaches soft-ball stage. Stir in pecans. Drop by spoonfuls onto a well-oiled piece of wax paper. Cool for 30 minutes and wrap individually.

Place in a decorative box or candy jar and use as a Valentine's Day gift.

Under 150 calories per candy
(Malt is a concentrated, high-carbohydrate food)

ENGLISH TOFFEE

Makes 64 candies

½ cup finely chopped nuts
½ cup butter
½ cup liquid barley malt

Sprinkle nuts over the bottom of a well-oiled 8-inch square pan. In a saucepan, melt butter, add malt and increase heat. Boil for 5 minutes until mixture reaches soft-ball stage. Pour butter-malt mixture over nuts. Cool slightly and mark off 1-inch squares. When completely cooled, break into pieces.

If placed in a decorative candy box, this toffee makes an excellent Valentine's Day gift.

Preparation and Cooking Time:
10 minutes
Cooling Time: 1 hour

Under 150 calories per candy
(Malt is a concentrated, high-carbohydrate food)

CREAM CHEESE NUT BONBONS

Makes 32 candies

8 ounces soft cream cheese
1 teaspoon almond extract ·
1 tablespoon frozen apple juice
   concentrate, thawed
2 tablespoons non-instant skim
   milk powder
1 cup finely chopped pecans or
   walnuts

Cream together cream cheese, almond extract, apple juice concentrate and milk powder to form a soft dough. If dough is sticky, add 1 tablespoon additional milk powder. Stir in nuts. With moistened hands, form into balls. Cover with plastic wrap and refrigerate overnight until firm.

This candy makes a lovely Valentine's Day gift if placed in a glass candy jar and decorated with a bow. Keep refrigerated.

Preparation Time: 10 minutes
Chilling Time: Overnight

Under 150 calories per candy
Under 20 grams carbohydrate per candy

MOCHA BALLS

Makes 24 candies

⅓ cup roasted carob powder

2 tablespoons grain coffee substitute

1 cup non-instant skim milk powder

⅓ cup soft butter

2 teaspoons vanilla

1 teaspoon roasted carob powder

1 tablespoon non-instant skim milk powder

2 teaspoons grain coffee substitute

In a bowl, mix carob powder, grain coffee and skim milk powder. Cream in butter to form a soft dough. Add vanilla. With moistened hands, form 24 balls.

In a small bowl, mix 1 teaspoon carob powder, 1 tablespoon non-instant milk powder and 2 teaspoon grain coffee. Roll balls in mixture to coat lightly. Cover with plastic wrap and refrigerate overnight until firm.

Place in a glass candy jar and decorate with a bow, if being used as a Valentine's Day gift. Keep candy refrigerated.

Preparation Time: 10 minutes
Chilling Time: Overnight

Under 150 calories per candy
Under 20 grams carbohydrate per candy

STRAWBERRY EGG NOG

Serves 8

4 cups milk

4 eggs, separated

1 cup frozen unsweetened strawberries, thawed

2 tablespoons frozen apple juice concentrate, thawed

In an electric blender or food processor, whip milk, egg yolks, strawberries and apple juice concentrate. Beat egg whites until stiff and fold into egg nog. Serve while still foamy.

Preparation Time: 10 minutes

Under 150 calories per serving
Approximately 20 grams carbohydrate per serving

ROSIE PUNCH

Serves 12 to 16

4 cups strawberry or strawberry-apple juice
3 cups mineral or seltzer water
2 cups whole unsweetened frozen strawberries

Combine juice and mineral water in a punch bowl.
Float frozen strawberries in sparkling juice.

Preparation Time: 5 minutes

Under 150 calories per serving
Approximately 20 grams carbohydrate per serving

Children's Valentine's Treats

JELLED HEARTS

Makes 12 3-inch hearts

3 envelopes unflavored gelatin
2¾ cups strawberry juice

Sprinkle gelatin over juice in a saucepan. Allow to
stand 5 minutes. Heat over low heat until dissolved.
Pour into a 9 x 12-inch pan and refrigerate for 2 to 3
hours until firmly set. Remove from refrigerator and
cut into heart shapes with a cookie cutter. Refrigerate
hearts when not being served. These holiday hearts
are firm enough to be eaten with fingers.

Preparation Time: 10 minutes
Chilling Time: 3 hours

Under 150 calories per heart
Under 30 grams carbohydrate per heart

HEART-SHAPED CARAMEL POPS
Makes 10 to 12 lollipops

¾ cup liquid barley malt
½ cup milk
½ cup non-instant skim milk
  powder

Preparation and Cooking Time:
15 minutes
Cooling Time: 15 minutes

In a saucepan, combine malt, milk and milk powder. Heat, stirring constantly, until mixture thickens. Continue to cook while stirring for 5 minutes. With moistened hands press mixture into well-oiled plastic Valentine cookie cutters. Press a stick into mixture while still warm. Cool for 15 minutes or until hard and lift lollipops out of the mold.

Approximately 225 calories per candy
(Malt is a concentrated, high-carbohydrate food)

FROZEN CAROB STRAWBERRIES
Makes 12 ounces coated strawberries

¼ cup coconut oil
3 tablespoons granular lecithin
⅓ cup roasted carob powder
⅓ cup non-instant skim milk
  powder
12 ounce package whole unsweetened frozen strawberries

Preparation Time: 20 minutes
Freezing Time: 1 hour

In a double boiler, melt coconut oil. Stir in lecithin and continue to cook until granules dissolve in oil. Stir in carob powder and milk powder 1 tablespoon at a time to form a smooth mixture. Place a toothpick in each strawberry. Dip strawberries in mixture and return to freezer. Eat directly from freezer.

Under 150 calories per strawberry
Under 20 grams carbohydrate per strawberry

STRAWBERRY HOT MILK
Serves 6

4 cups milk
1 tablespoon strawberry con-
    centrate
1 cup heavy cream
1 teaspoon almond extract

Heat milk in a saucepan. Stir in strawberry concentrate and pour into mugs. Whip cream and almond extract. Spoon on top of each serving.

Preparation and Cooking Time:
10 minutes

Over 250 calories per serving
Under 30 grams carbohydrate per serving

6

Heavenly
Easter Goodies

PEACH TRIFLE

Serves 10

Half stale Lemon Loaf (see p. 102) cut in 1-inch cubes
1 16-ounce can sliced cling peaches in juice
1 tablespoon cornstarch
⅔ cup sherry
1¼ cups milk
2 tablespoons cornstarch
3 egg yolks
1 tablespoon frozen apple juice concentrate, thawed
1 teaspoon vanilla
1 cup heavy cream
½ teaspoon almond extract

Preparation and Cooking Time: 1 hour

Place cake cubes in a large bowl. In a saucepan, combine juice from canned peaches and 1 tablespoon cornstarch. Heat, stirring constantly, until thickened. Stir in sherry and remove from heat. Pour over cake. Allow to marinate for 40 minutes.

In a saucepan, combine milk, 2 tablespoons cornstarch, egg yolks and apple juice concentrate. Cook over medium heat, stirring occasionally without bringing to a boil, until mixture thickens to a custard. Stir in vanilla and cool.

Beat together heavy cream and almond extract. Fold custard into cake mixture. Stir in peaches. Fold cream into trifle. Serve immediately or chill until time to serve.

Over 250 calories per serving
Over 35 grams carbohydrate per serving

MOLASSES MARBLE CAKE WITH LEMON SAUCE   *Serves 9*

MOLASSES BATTER INGRE-
DIENTS

3 tablespoons oil
⅔ cup apple juice
2 eggs, separated
3 tablespoons blackstrap molasses
2 teaspoons baking powder
½ cup whole wheat pastry flour
½ cup brown rice flour
¼ cup non-instant milk powder
½ teaspoon cinnamon
½ teaspoon ground ginger

BLOND BATTER INGREDIENTS

3 tablespoons oil
⅔ cup apple juice
¼ cup liquid barley malt
2 teaspoons lemon juice
2 teaspoons grated lemon peel
2 eggs, separated

½ cup whole wheat pastry flour
½ cup brown rice flour
3 tablespoons non-instant skim
    milk powder
1 teaspoon baking soda

LEMON SAUCE

1 cup apple juice
1 tablespoon lemon juice

To make molasses batter, combine oil, apple juice, egg yolks, and molasses. In a separate bowl, mix baking powder, whole wheat pastry flour, brown rice flour, milk powder, cinnamon and ginger until well combined. Gradually beat dry mixture into liquid ingredients to form a smooth batter. Beat egg whites until stiff. Fold into batter and set aside.

To make blond batter, combine oil, apple juice, liquid barley malt, lemon juice, lemon peel and egg yolks. In a separate bowl, mix pastry flour, rice flour, milk powder and baking soda. Gradually stir dry mixture into liquid ingredients to form a smooth batter. Beat egg whites until stiff. Fold into batter.

Preheat oven to 350 degrees. Pour blond batter into oiled 8-inch square pan. Spoon molasses batter into 4 corners of blond batter. With a kitchen knife, swirl batters to form a marble effect. Bake for 1 hour until a toothpick inserted into the center of the cake comes out clean. Turn cake onto a rack to cool.

To make lemon sauce, combine apple juice, lemon juice, lemon peel and cornstarch in a saucepan. Heat, stirring constantly, until mixture thickens. Reduce heat to low. To make whipped topping, blend ricotta, lemon juice, apple juice concentrate, lemon peel and vanilla in an electric blender or food processor until smooth.

Cut cake into 9 squares, spoon over warm lemon sauce and top with ricotta topping. Serve immediately.

1 tablespoon grated lemon peel
1 tablespoon cornstarch

WHIPPED TOPPING
¾ cup part-skim milk ricotta
  cheese
½ teaspoon lemon juice
1 tablespoon frozen apple juice
  concentrate, thawed
1 tablespoon grated lemon peel
½ teaspoon vanilla

Preparation Time: 25 minutes
Baking Time: 1 hour

Over 250 calories per serving
Over 35 grams carbohydrate per serving

GLORIFIED PINEAPPLE RICE

Serves 8

1 cup cooked brown rice or
  sweet rice
1 16-ounce can crushed unsweetened pineapple, drained
1 teaspoon vanilla
1 cup part-skim milk ricotta
  cheese
2 tablespoons pineapple juice,
  reserved from crushed pineapple

Mix rice, pineapple and vanilla. In an electric blender or food processor blend ricotta and pineapple juice until smooth. Fold into rice and pineapple mixture.

Preparation Time: 10 minutes

Under 150 calories per serving
Over 35 grams carbohydrate per serving

CRÊPES SUZETTE

Serves 9

Delicate Whole Wheat Crêpes
  or Low Calorie Eggless
  Crêpes recipe (see p. 18)
1 tablespoon butter
1 cup fresh orange juice
1 teaspoon grated orange peel
4 teaspoons cornstarch
½ teaspoon vanilla

Preparation and Cooking Time:
30 minutes

Prepare crêpes. In a skillet, melt butter and add orange juice, orange peel, cornstarch and vanilla. Heat, stirring constantly, until thickened. Place crêpes in sauce one at a time and turn, coating each crêpe with sauce. Fold in quarters and place on plates to serve.

Under 150 calories per serving
Under 30 grams carbohydrate per serving

EASTER BREAKFAST BLINTZES

Serves 9

Delicate Whole Wheat Crêpes
  or Low Calorie Eggless
  Crêpes recipe (see p. 18)

FILLING INGREDIENTS
1½ cups part-skim milk ricotta
  cheese
1 tablespoon frozen apple juice
  concentrate, thawed
1 teaspoon vanilla

SAUCE INGREDIENTS
1 cup apple juice
1 tablespoon cornstarch
1 teaspoon ground cardamom

Preparation and Cooking Time:
40 minutes

Prepare crêpes. In a blender or food processor, blend ricotta, apple juice concentrate and vanilla. Spoon a tablespoon of filling in a line across the center of each crêpe. Roll crêpes around filling. For sauce ingredients, heat apple juice, cornstarch and cardamom in a saucepan until thickened. Pour sauce over crêpes just before serving.

Under 150 calories per serving
Under 30 grams carbohydrate per serving

BANANA CRÊPES
Serves 9

Delicate Whole Wheat Crêpes
or Low Calorie Eggless
Crêpes recipe (see p. 18)

FILLING INGREDIENTS
2 ripe bananas, sliced
1 tablespoon pineapple juice
½ teaspoon cinnamon

SAUCE INGREDIENTS
1 cup pineapple juice
1 tablespoon cornstarch
1 teaspoon vanilla

*Preparation and Cooking Time:
40 minutes*

Prepare crêpes. In a blender or food processor, blend bananas, pineapple juice and cinnamon until smooth. Place 1 tablespoon of filling across the center of each crêpe in a line. Roll crêpes. For sauce ingredients, heat pineapple juice, starch and vanilla in a saucepan until thickened. Pour sauce over crêpes just before serving.

Under 150 calories per serving
Under 30 grams carbohydrate per serving

PINEAPPLE SOUFFLÉ
Serves 12

1 cup crushed unsweetened
pineapple, drained
2 envelopes unflavored gelatin
1¾ cups pineapple juice
8 eggs, separated
1½ cups chilled heavy cream

Line the bottom of a 6-cup soufflé dish with pineapple. Extend top of soufflé with a 2-inch band of heavy duty aluminum foil, secured with a string. In a saucepan, sprinkle gelatin over pineapple juice. Let stand 5 minutes. Beat in egg yolks and cook over low heat, stirring occasionally, for 5 minutes until gelatin dissolves and mixture thickens slightly. Refrigerate for 30 minutes until mixture has the consistency of custard, but is not set. Beat egg whites until stiff and glossy. Fold into gelatin mixture. Beat cream until fluffy and fold into egg and gelatin mixture. Turn into soufflé dish and refrigerate for 8 hours until firm.

Preparation Time: 15 minutes
Chilling Time: 8 hours

Approximately 225 calories per serving
Approximately 20 grams carbohydrate per serving

ORANGE BAKED SOUFFLÉ

Serves 10

1 tablespoon butter
¼ cup whole wheat pastry flour
   or soy flour
½ cup milk
7 eggs, separated
⅓ cup frozen orange juice concentrate, thawed
1 tablespoon grated orange peel
¼ teaspoon cream of tartar

Preheat oven to 375 degrees. In a saucepan, melt butter. In a bowl, beat flour and milk until smooth. Stir into melted butter and cook until mixture thickens and there is no taste of raw flour. Remove from heat and beat in egg yolks. Return to low heat and stir until thickened. Remove from heat and stir in orange juice and orange peel. Cool.

Beat egg whites and cream of tartar until stiff and glossy. Fold into orange mixture. Extend a 2-quart soufflé dish with 2 inches of heavy duty aluminum foil, and secure with a string. Butter soufflé dish and foil. Turn soufflé mixture into dish and bake for 40 to 50 minutes until golden brown.

Preparation Time: 20 minutes
Baking Time: 40 to 50 minutes

Under 150 calories per serving
Approximately 20 grams carbohydrate per serving

CRÈME DE MENTHE SOUFFLÉ

Serves 10

3 envelopes unflavored gelatin
¾ cup pineapple juice
3 cups milk
4 tablespoons cornstarch
8 eggs, separated
3 tablespoons natural crème de
   menthe extract

Sprinkle gelatin over pineapple juice. In a saucepan combine milk, cornstarch and egg yolks. Cook over medium heat, stirring occasionally, until mixture thickens. Remove from heat and stir in crème de menthe extract, and gelatin in pineapple juice. Chill just until mixture is the consistency of custard but is not set, about 1 hour.

Extend a 6-cup soufflé dish with a 2-inch strip of aluminum foil secured with a string. Beat egg whites until stiff and glossy. Fold into jelled mixtured and turn into soufflé. Chill for 8 hours until firm. Run a knife around the edge of the foil extension and remove before serving.

Preparation Time: 25 minutes
Chilling Time: 9 hours

Under 150 calories per serving
Approximately 20 grams carbohydrate per serving

BAKED APRICOT SOUFFLÉ

Serves 10

1 cup dried apricots
1 cup water
½ cup frozen apple juice concentrate, thawed
2 tablespoons soy flour
6 eggs, separated
¼ teaspoon cream of tartar

In a saucepan, combine apricots and water. Cook over medium heat for 30 minutes until soft. Blend in an electric blender or food processor until smooth. Return to pan and add apple juice concentrate and soy flour. Cook, stirring occasionally, until there is no taste of raw flour. Stir in egg yolks and cook without boiling for 2 minutes. Remove from heat and cool. Preheat oven to 375 degrees.

Beat egg whites until stiff and fold into apricot mixture. Turn into a buttered 2-quart soufflé dish and bake for 40 to 45 minutes until golden brown.

Preparation Time: 45 minutes
Baking Time: 40 to 45 minutes

Under 150 calories per serving
Approximately 25 grams carbohydrate per serving

PIÑA COLADA MERINGUE PIE

Serves 8

½ Flaky Pastry Dough or
  Stretchy Pastry Dough recipe
  (see p. 16)
4 tablespoons arrowroot starch
  or cornstarch
4 tablespoons brown rice flour
½ cup pineapple juice
1¼ cups boiling coconut juice
4 eggs, separated
2 teaspoons frozen pineapple
  juice concentrate, thawed
1 tablespoon unsweetened
  shredded coconut

Preparation Time: 20 minutes
Baking Time: 15 minutes

Preheat oven to 350 degrees. Prepare dough and line a 9-inch pie plate. Bake for 15 minutes. Cool.

To prepare filling, mix starch, rice flour and pineapple juice in a saucepan. Place over medium heat and gradually stir in boiling coconut juice. Continue stirring until mixture thickens. Beat in egg yolks and remove from heat. Pour into pie shell. Beat egg whites until foamy. Add pineapple juice concentrate and beat until stiff and glossy. Pile in a decorative manner over pie. Sprinkle with coconut and bake for 15 minutes until meringue is lightly browned on top peaks. Do not overcook. Cool before serving.

Under 150 calories per serving
Approximately 20 grams carbohydrate per serving

MINT CAROB LAYERED DESSERT

Serves 10 to 12

Crumble Crust recipe (see p. 17)

CAROB LAYER INGREDIENTS
1 envelope unflavored gelatin
¼ cup strong peppermint tea,
  cooled
1 cup roasted carob powder
1 cup milk

Make crust and press into a 9-inch springform pan and refrigerate.

To make carob layer, sprinkle gelatin over peppermint tea, and set aside. In a saucepan, combine carob powder, milk and rice flour. Cook over medium heat, stirring occasionally until mixture thickens. Stir in gelatin mixture and remove from heat. Refrigerate until mixture reaches the consistency of custard but is not set, about 40 minutes.

2 tablespoons brown rice flour

2 egg whites

MINT LAYER
1 envelope unflavored gelatin
½ cup strong peppermint tea,
    cooled
1 cup part-skim milk ricotta
    cheese
2 tablespoons frozen apple
    juice concentrate, thawed
2 egg whites

GARNISH
1 3-ounce Burry's Health Food
    Carob Mint Bar, grated

Preparation Time: 20 minutes
Chilling Time: 8 hours

Beat egg whites until stiff and fold in. Spread mixture evenly over crust and return to refrigerator while preparing mint layer.

To make mint layer, sprinkle gelatin over peppermint tea in a saucepan. Heat over low heat just until gelatin dissolves. Remove from heat and pour into an electric blender jar. Add ricotta and apple juice concentrate. Blend until smooth. Pour into a bowl and refrigerate until mixture is the consistency of custard but not set, about 40 minutes.

Beat egg whites until stiff and fold into chilled mint mixture. Pour over carob layer and spread evenly. Sprinkle with grated carob bar. Chill in the refrigerator for 6 hours until stiff. Run a knife around the edge of the pan and remove springform.

Under 150 calories per serving
Approximately 20 grams carbohydrate per serving

ORANGE BAVARIAN

Serves 8

½ cup boiling water
1 envelope unflavored gelatin
1½ cups fresh orange juice
1 tablespoon grated orange peel
1 cup part-skim milk ricotta
    cheese
1 tablespoon frozen apple juice
    concentrate, thawed
2 egg whites

Preparation Time: 20 minutes
Chilling Time: 5 hours

Pour boiling water over gelatin. Let stand 5 minutes until gelatin is dissolved. Stir in orange juice and grated orange peel. Refrigerate for 30 minutes until mixture mounds. Remove from refrigerator and beat until fluffy. In an electric blender, blend ricotta and apple juice concentrate. Fold into gelatin mixture. Beat egg whites until stiff and fold into gelatin and ricotta mixture. Turn into a 4-cup gelatin mold and refrigerate for 4 to 5 hours until firm. Unmold to serve.

Under 150 calories per serving
Approximately 20 grams carbohydrate per serving

COFFEE JELLY

Serves 4

3 teaspoons grain coffee substi-
    tute
1 envelope unflavored gelatin
2 cups boiling apple juice
1 teaspoon vanilla
1 cup light cream or milk (op-
    tional)

Preparation Time: 5 minutes
Chilling Time: 3 hours

Sprinkle coffee substitute and gelatin over boiling juice. Let stand 5 minutes until dissolved, and stir in vanilla. Pour into a 2-cup gelatin mold and chill for 3 hours until firm. If desired serve with milk or cream.

Under 150 calories per serving
Under 20 grams carbohydrate per serving

PINEAPPLE CHIFFON PIE

Serves 8

½ Flaky Pastry Dough or
    Stretchy Pastry Dough (see
    p. 16)
1 envelope unflavored gelatin
⅓ cup pineapple juice
4 eggs, separated
1 cup milk
1 tablespoon cornstarch
1 cup canned unsweetened pin-
    eapple, drained

Preparation Time: 20 minutes
Chilling Time: 4 hours

Preheat oven to 375 degrees. Prepare dough and line a 9-inch pie plate. Bake for 15 minutes until browned.
    Sprinkle gelatin over pineapple juice and set aside. In a saucepan, combine egg yolks, milk, cornstarch and drained pineapple. Heat without boiling, stirring occasionally, until mixture thickens. Stir in gelatin and pineapple juice and remove from heat. Chill until mixture mounds, about 30 minutes. Remove from refrigerator and beat with a wire whisk until fluffy. Beat egg whites until stiff and fold in. Turn into baked pie shell and chill for 3 hours until set.

Under 150 calories per serving
Approximately 20 grams carbohydrate per serving

PINEAPPLE PARFAITS

Serves 6 to 8

1 envelope unflavored gelatin
1 cup boiling pineapple juice
1 cup part-skim milk ricotta cheese
3 eggs, separated
1 16-ounce can crushed unsweetened pineapple
1 tablespoon cornstarch or arrowroot starch

Sprinkle gelatin over boiling pineapple juice and dissolve. Pour into a blender with ricotta and blend until smooth. Refrigerate until mixture mounds, about 30 minutes. Beat egg whites until stiff and fold into mixture. Return to refrigerator.

In a saucepan, combine egg yolks, the pineapple with its juice and starch. Heat, stirring occasionally, until mixture thickens. Remove from heat and allow to cool. Remove jelled mixture from refrigerator. Alternate layers of jelled ricotta mixture and thickened pineapple in parfait glasses. Refrigerate for 2 hours until ready to serve.

Preparation Time: 20 minutes
Chilling Time: 3 hours

Under 150 calories
Approximately 25 grams carbohydrate per serving

BROILED GRAPEFRUIT

Serves 4

2 grapefruits
4 tablespoons frozen apple juice concentrate, thawed

Slice grapefruits in half and cut fruit away from membranes for serving. Drizzle each half with 1 tablespoon apple juice concentrate. Brown fruit for fifteen minutes, 3 to 4 inches from oven broiler.

Preparation Time: 10 minutes
Baking Time: 15 minutes

Under 150 calories per serving
Approximately 20 grams carbohydrate per serving

OLD-FASHIONED JELLY ROLL

Serves 9

1 large ripe banana
3 eggs, separated
2 tablespoons whole wheat
   pastry flour
2 tablespoons brown rice flour
¼ teaspoon baking powder
1 tablespoon frozen apple juice
   concentrate, thawed

½ cup ground nuts
⅔ cup unsweetened fruit preserves

Preparation Time: 15 minutes
Baking Time: 15 minutes
Assembling Time: 10 minutes

Preheat oven to 375 degrees. In an electric blender, purée banana and egg yolks. In a bowl, combine flours and baking powder. Stir in purée to form a smooth batter. Beat egg whites until stiff, then beat in apple juice concentrate. Fold mixture into batter. Grease a 9 x 13-inch jelly roll pan. Line with wax paper and grease paper. Pour batter into pan and bake 15 minutes.

Sprinkle nuts over a clean kitchen towel. Turn cake onto towel. Carefully remove wax paper. Trim edges of cake for easy rolling. Spread preserves over the whole surface of the cake and roll. Set seam side down to cool. Cut into 1-inch slices to serve.

Approximately 225 calories per serving
Approximately 30 grams carbohydrate per serving

ÉCLAIRS

Makes 18

Cream Puff Pastry recipe (see
   p. 19)

CUSTARD INGREDIENTS
4 tablespoons cornstarch or arrowroot starch
2 cups milk
3 egg yolks
2 teaspoons vanilla
3 tablespoons frozen apple
   juice concentrate, thawed

Preheat oven to 425 degrees. Spoon cream puff batter onto a baking sheet sprayed with nonstick vegetable spray in long, thinly shaped tablespoonfuls. Bake for 45 minutes until golden brown. Turn off heat and allow puffs to cool in oven

To make custard, combine cornstarch, milk, egg yolks, vanilla and apple juice concentrate in a saucepan. Cook over medium heat, stirring occasionally, until mixture thickens. Remove from heat and cool.

To make frosting, blend butter, carob powder and water in an electric blender or food processor until

FROSTING INGREDIENTS
3 tablespoons soft butter
1 cup roasted carob powder
⅓ cup water

Preparation Time: 30 minutes
Baking Time: 45 minutes
Assembling Time: 15 minutes

smooth and thick. To assemble, cut éclairs in half, spoon in custard and frost.

Approximately 225 calories per serving
Approximately 20 grams carbohydrate per serving

APPLE BUTTER DOUGHNUTS   *Serves 24*

1 tablespoon baking yeast
¾ cup warm apple juice
3 tablespoons apple butter
2 tablespoons oil
½ cup orange juice
4 cups whole wheat pastry flour
3 tablespoons gluten flour
1 teaspoon cinnamon
Oil for frying

Sprinkle yeast over warm apple juice and allow to stand 10 minutes until dissolved. Stir in apple butter, oil and orange juice. In a separate bowl, mix flours, and cinnamon. Gradually beat flour mixture into liquids with a wooden spoon to form a soft dough. Knead on a floured surface for 10 minutes until smooth and elastic. Wrap in plastic wrap or wax paper and refrigerate for 30 minutes, until firm.

Roll out dough to ¼-inch thickness and cut with doughnut cutters. Place on an oiled surface in a warm place, cover with a towel and allow to rise for 45 minutes until light and spongy. Heat 3 inches of oil to 375 degrees and fry doughnuts on both sides until browned. Drain on paper towels.

These doughnuts can be served immediately or given as a gift. Placed in a decorative tin with a note that homemade doughnuts are best served hot and can be heated in a 300 degree oven just before serving, they make a wonderful Easter surprise.

Preparation Time: 1½ hours
Frying Time: 20 minutes

Approximately 225 calories per serving
Over 35 grams carbohydrate per serving

LEMON DOUGHNUTS

Serves 24

DOUGH INGREDIENTS

1 tablespoon baking yeast
1 cup warm orange juice
3 tablespoons frozen apple
  juice concentrate, thawed
1 teaspoon vanilla
2 tablespoons safflower oil
2 tablespoons lemon juice
1 tablespoon grated lemon peel

3 tablespoons gluten flour
3½ cups whole wheat pastry
  flour

GLAZE INGREDIENTS

1 cup apple juice
1 tablespoon lemon juice
1 tablespoon lemon peel
2 tablespoons arrowroot starch
  dissolved in 2 tablespoons
  water

Preparation Time: 1½ hours
Frying Time: 20 minutes

Sprinkle yeast over warm orange juice and let stand 10 minutes until yeast is dissolved. Stir in apple juice concentrate, vanilla, oil, lemon juice and lemon peel.

In a bowl, mix gluten flour and whole wheat pastry flour. Gradually beat flours into liquid mixture with a wooden spoon to form a soft dough. Knead on a floured surface until smooth and elastic. Cover and refrigerate for 30 minutes until firm. Roll out dough to ¼-inch thickness and cut into doughnut shapes with a doughnut cutter. Place on an oiled surface, cover with a towel and let rise 40 minutes until light and spongy.

Heat 3 inches of oil to 375 degrees and fry doughnuts on both sides until golden brown. Drain on paper towels.

To make glaze, heat apple juice, lemon juice and lemon peel to boiling. Stir in starch-and-water combination for 3 minutes until thickened. Spoon a light coating over doughnuts.

These festive Easter doughnuts can be eaten immediately or given as a present. For a gift, place doughnuts in a foil-lined Easter basket with a note saying that doughnuts are best if reheated for 10 minutes in a 300 degree oven.

Approximately 225 calories per serving
Over 35 grams carbohydrate per serving

LEMON LOAF

Serves 12 to 16

LOAF INGREDIENTS

⅓ cup oil or soft unsalted butter

½ cup apple juice

¼ cup liquid barley malt

3 eggs

2 tablespoons lemon juice

⅓ cup non-instant skim milk powder

1 tablespoon grated lemon peel

1 cup whole wheat pastry flour

¾ cup brown rice flour

1 teaspoon baking soda

FROSTING INGREDIENTS

1 tablespoon soft butter

⅓ cup non-instant skim milk powder

½ teaspoon grated lemon peel

1 tablespoon lemon juice

3 tablespoons apple juice

Preparation Time: 15 minutes
Baking Time: 1 hour

Preheat oven to 350 degrees. In a bowl, mix oil, apple juice, malt, eggs, lemon juice, non-instant milk powder and lemon peel until smooth.

In a separate bowl, mix pastry flour, brown rice flour and baking soda with a wire whisk. Gradually stir flour mixture into liquid to form a smooth batter. Pour into a well-oiled loaf pan and bake for 1 hour until a toothpick inserted into the center of the cake comes out clean. Remove from pan and cool on a wire rack.

To make frosting blend soft butter, milk powder, lemon peel, lemon juice and apple juice in an electric blender or food processor until smooth. Drizzle frosting over loaf so that it drips over sides. Allow to stand until frosting becomes firm.

This loaf makes a wonderful Easter breakfast food or gift. As a gift, place in a square Easter basket lined with foil and decorated with a bow.

Approximately 225 calories per serving
Approximately 30 grams carbohydrate per serving

PINEAPPLE BREAD

Serves 12 to 16

LOAF INGREDIENTS
1 cup whole wheat pastry flour
¾ cup brown rice flour
⅓ cup non-instant milk powder
1 to 2 teaspoons baking powder
⅓ cup oil
¾ cup pineapple juice
3 eggs
¼ cup liquid barley malt
¾ cup crushed canned unsweetened pineapple, drained

FROSTING INGREDIENTS
1 tablespoon soft butter
⅓ cup non-instant skim milk
   powder
¼ cup pineapple juice

Preparation Time: 15 minutes
Baking Time: 1 hour

Preheat oven to 350 degrees. In a bowl, mix pastry flour, brown rice flour, milk powder and baking powder with a wire whisk.

In a separate bowl, beat oil, pineapple juice, eggs, barley malt and crushed pineapple. Gradually stir flour mixture into liquids to form a smooth batter. Pour into a well-oiled loaf pan and bake for 1 hour until a toothpick inserted into the center comes out clean. Remove from pan and cool on a wire rack.

To make frosting, blend butter, milk powder and pineapple juice in an electic blender or food processor until smooth. Frost cake.

This recipe can be used as a party food or as a gift. As an Easter gift, line a rectangular Easter basket with foil, tie a bow on the handle and place Pineapple Bread in basket.

Approximately 225 calories per serving
Over 35 grams carbohydrate per serving

ORANGE CINNAMON ROLLS

Serves 16

DOUGH INGREDIENTS
1 tablespoon baking yeast
1¼ cups warm orange juice
2 tablespoons frozen apple
   juice concentrate, thawed
4 teaspoons grated orange peel
2 eggs, beaten

Sprinkle yeast over warm orange juice. Let stand for 10 minutes until dissolved. Stir in apple juice concentrate, orange peel and eggs. In a separate bowl, combine pastry flour, gluten flour and soy flour, stirring with a wire whisk. Gradually beat 1¾ cups of flour mixture into liquids to form a sponge. Cover and allow to rise in a warm place until foamy, about 20 minutes.

2¼ cups whole wheat pastry
flour
¾ cup gluten flour
¾ cup soy flour

ORANGE GLAZE INGREDIENTS
1 cup orange juice
1½ tablespoons cornstarch or
arrowroot starch
1 tablespoon grated orange peel
½ teaspoon cinnamon

Beat in remaining flour with a wooden spoon to form a soft dough. Knead for 10 minutes on a lightly floured board until smooth and elastic. If dough becomes sticky, knead in additional whole wheat pastry flour. Cover and refrigerate dough for 1½ hours until firm.

Form dough into 16 desired roll shapes. Place on an oiled surface in a warm place, cover and allow to rise until doubled in bulk, about 1 hour. Preheat oven to 350 degrees and bake for 30 minutes until golden brown.

To make glaze, combine orange juice and cornstarch in a saucepan. Heat to boiling, stirring constantly, and add orange peel and cinnamon. Remove from heat and cool to warm. Spread a light layer over each roll.

Served warm, these rolls make a lovely party or breakfast food. They can also make a delicious gift food if placed in a foil-lined Easter basket.

Preparation Time: 3 to 4 hours
Baking Time: 30 minutes

Approximately 150 calories per serving
Over 35 grams carbohydrate per serving

EASTER BREAD
Serves 15

1 tablespoon baking yeast
1 cup warm pineapple juice
¼ cup frozen pineapple juice
concentrate, thawed
¼ cup melted butter
2 eggs, beaten
2⅓ cups whole wheat pastry
flour
¾ cup soy flour
¾ cup gluten flour

Sprinkle yeast over warm pineapple juice and let stand for 10 minutes until dissolved. Beat in pineapple juice concentrate, melted butter and eggs. In a separate bowl, combine flours, cinnamon, raisins, dates and pineapple.

Using a wooden spoon, beat flours into liquid mixture to form a soft dough. Knead for 10 minutes on a floured surface until smooth and elastic. If dough becomes sticky, knead in additional flour. Oil dough and place in a bowl in a warm place, covered with a warm,

1 teaspoon cinnamon
½ cup raisins
¼ cup chopped dates
¼ cup chopped dried pineapple
2 egg yolks beaten with 1 tablespoon pineapple juice

damp towel, to rise until doubled in bulk, about 1½ hours. Punch down and place in an oiled loaf pan, cover, and set in a warm place to rise until doubled in bulk again, about 1 hour. Preheat oven to 325 degrees.

Beat 2 egg yolks with 1 tablespoon pineapple juice and brush over dough. Place in oven to bake for 45 minutes until lightly browned.

Served warm, Easter Bread is a delicious party or breakfast food. To use as a gift, wrap in pink or yellow cellophane and tie with a bow.

Preparation Time: 3 to 4 hours
Baking Time: 45 minutes

Approximately 225 calories per serving
Over 35 grams carbohydrate per serving

NUT-FILLED HORNS

Makes 4 dozen

1 tablespoon baking yeast
1 cup warm apple juice
3 tablespoons frozen apple
   juice concentrate, thawed
2 tablespoons oil
4 eggs, separated
2¼ cups whole wheat pastry
   flour
¾ cup gluten flour
¾ cup soy flour
1 tablespoon frozen apple juice
   concentrate, thawed
1 cup chopped walnuts

Sprinkle yeast over warm apple juice and let stand for 10 minutes until dissolved and bubbly. Stir in apple juice concentrate, oil and egg yolks.

In a separate bowl, mix whole wheat flour, gluten flour and soy flour. Beat 2 cups of flour mixture into liquids to form a sponge. Cover and let rise in a warm place for 20 minutes until foamy. Beat down with a wooden spoon and beat in remaining flour to form a soft dough. Knead for 10 minutes until smooth and elastic. Cover and set in a warm place to rise for 1½ hours. Roll dough ⅛-inch thick and cut into 2½-inch squares. Place squares on an oiled surface, in a warm place and let rise for 1 hour until doubled in bulk.

Beat egg whites until stiff. Beat in 1 tablespoon apple juice concentrate. Fold in walnuts. Place 1 teaspoon of egg white-walnut mixture in the center of each square of dough. Fold two adjoining edges of dough over filling and join them to form a conelike shape. Preheat oven to 400 degrees and bake for 20 minutes until golden brown.

Served directly from the oven, Nut-Filled Horns are a festive party or breakfast food. They also make a delicious gift if placed in a foil-lined Easter basket.

Preparation Time: 3 to 4 hours
Baking Time: 20 minutes

Approximately 225 calories per serving
Over 35 grams carbohydrate per serving

MERINGUE MUSHROOMS

Serves 24

3 egg whites
½ teaspoon cream of tartar
3 tablespoons liquid barley malt
3 tablespoons water

Preheat oven to 200 degrees. Beat egg whites with cream of tartar until foamy. In a separate saucepan, combine malt and water. Bring to a boil and continue to boil for 15 minutes until mixture reaches soft-ball stage. While malt mixture cooks, continue to beat egg whites until stiff and glossy. Gradually pour malt mixture into egg whites. Beat again until dense and glossy.

Spray a baking sheet with nonstick vegetable spray. Spoon meringue into a pastry decorator's bag. Using a plain ½-inch tip, make mushroom caps by pressing out mounds of meringue about 1½ inches in diameter. To make stems, press out 1¼-inch lengths of meringue. Bake for 40 minutes until completely dried out and golden. To assemble mushrooms, turn caps upside down and cut a small hole with a sharp knife. Moisten finger with water and wet small end of stem lightly, then press gently into cap hole.

These fancy little mushrooms make a lovely gift if arranged in a basket of Easter grass.

Preparation Time: 15 minutes
Baking Time: 40 minutes

Under 150 calories per serving
Under 30 grams carbohydrate per serving

HOT CROSS BUNS

Serves 30 to 36

DOUGH INGREDIENTS

2 tablespoons baking yeast
2 cups warm apple juice
6 tablespoons melted butter
2 eggs, beaten
1 cup frozen apple juice concentrate, thawed
1 cup raisins
4½ cups whole wheat pastry
   flour
1½ cups soy flour
1½ cups gluten flour

FROSTING INGREDIENTS

2 tablespoons soft butter
¾ cup non-instant skim milk
   powder
½ cup apple juice

Sprinkle yeast over warm apple juice. Let stand for 10 minutes until dissolved. Stir in melted butter, eggs, apple juice concentrate and raisins. In a separate bowl, mix pastry flour, soy flour and gluten flour with a wire whisk. Gradually beat 3 cups of flour mixture into liquids to form a sponge. Cover and set in a warm place to rise for 20 minutes until doubled. With a wooden spoon, beat in remaining flour mixture to form a soft dough. Turn onto a floured board and knead for 10 minutes until smooth and elastic. Place in an oiled bowl and oil top of dough. Cover and let rise in a warm place for about 1½ hours until doubled in bulk. Punch down and form dough into 30 to 36 egg-shaped rolls. Place on oiled baking sheet, cover and let rise in a warm place for about 1 hour until doubled in bulk. Preheat oven to 325 degrees and bake buns for 25 minutes until lightly browned.

To make frosting, blend butter, milk powder and apple juice in an electric blender or food processor until smooth. Place frosting in a pastry bag with a ¼-inch plain tip and make a cross on each roll.

These traditional buns make a distinctive party breakfast food when served warm. They also make a lovely gift if placed in a foil-lined Easter basket or decorative cake tin.

Preparation Time: 3 to 4 hours
Baking Time: 25 minutes

Approximately 150 calories per serving
Over 35 grams carbohydrate per serving

PINEAPPLE TEA RINGS

Serves 20

DOUGH INGREDIENTS

2 tablespoons baking yeast
2 cups warm pineapple juice
3 tablespoons melted butter
2 eggs, beaten
½ cup frozen pineapple juice concentrate, thawed
4½ cups whole wheat pastry flour
1½ cups gluten flour
1½ cups soy flour

FILLING INGREDIENTS

1 16-ounce can unsweetened crushed pineapple, drained
1 tablespoon cornstarch
½ cup unsweetened shredded coconut
1 egg beaten with 1 tablespoon frozen pineapple juice concentrate

Sprinkle yeast over warm pineapple juice and let stand for 10 minutes until dissolved. Beat in melted butter, eggs, and pineapple juice concentrate. In a separate bowl, combine pastry flour, gluten flour and soy flour, mixing well with a wire whisk. Gradually beat flour mixture into liquids with a wooden spoon to form a soft dough. Knead on a floured board for 10 minutes until smooth and elastic. Form into a ball. Oil. Place in a covered bowl and set in a warm place for 1½ hours until double in bulk. Divide into two portions. Roll each portion into 12 x 20-inch rectangles.

To make filling, mix drained pineapple, cornstarch and coconut in a bowl and spread a layer over each rectangle. Roll in jelly roll fashion. Bring ends around to form a circle and seal seam with moistened fingers.

With a sharp knife or pastry scissors, cut rings 1½ inches apart from the outside of the rings toward the center, without cutting through the center. Cover and let rise for 1½ hours until doubled in bulk. Preheat oven to 350 degrees. Brush dough with egg and pineapple juice concentrate mixture and bake for 30 minutes until golden brown. If desired, frost rings with frosting used for Hot Cross Buns. (See previous recipe.)

Served warm, these rings make a festive party food. They also make a lovely gift if placed in round decorative tins or in round, foil-lined Easter baskets.

Preparation Time: 3 to 4 hours
Baking Time: 30 minutes

Approximately 225 calories per serving
Over 35 grams carbohydrate per serving

MERINGUE CAFÉ AU LAIT

Serves 4 to 6

4 teaspoons grain coffee substitute

2 cups milk

2 cups water

2 egg whites

2 teaspoons frozen apple juice concentrate, thawed

½ teaspoon grain coffee substitute

In a saucepan, heat grain coffee substitute, milk and water. To make meringue, beat egg whites until stiff, then beat in apple juice concentrate and coffee substitute. Pour coffee into cups and spoon meringue on top.

Preparation and Cooking Time: 10 minutes

Under 150 calories per serving
Under 20 grams carbohydrate per serving

FANCY MOCHA

Serves 4 to 6

3 teaspoons grain coffee substitute

2 teaspoons roasted carob powder

3 cups water

1 cup milk

2 egg whites

½ teaspoon vanilla

In a pan, heat grain coffee substitute, carob powder, water and milk. Beat egg whites until stiff and blend in vanilla. Pour hot mocha into cups and spoon meringue on top just before serving.

Preparation and Cooking Time: 10 minutes

Under 150 calories per serving
Under 20 grams carbohydrate per serving

Children's Easter Treats

BIG POPCORN BUNNY

Makes 1 12-inch rabbit

½ cup popcorn kernels
2 tablespoons safflower oil
½ cup liquid barley malt
¼ cup safflower oil
3 raisins
1 cashew

Pop corn in 2 tablespoons safflower oil. In a large pot, heat malt and ¼ cup safflower oil until bubbling. Stir in popped corn until thoroughly coated. Cool only until mixture can be handled.

To shape bunny, place 3 cups of malted popcorn on an oiled dinner plate. With moistened hands, form popcorn into a mound that is 5 inches high and 4 inches at the base and 2 inches at the top. Stick 3 toothpicks halfway into the top of the mound. Measure 1 cup of popcorn and form a ball for the rabbit's head. Press ball into toothpicks. Press two raisins into the ball for eyes, and one for a nose. Press the cashew under the nose for a mouth. Measure ½ cup popcorn for each ear and form oblong shapes. Insert two toothpicks into each side of the head and press ears onto these toothpicks. With ¼ cup popcorn form a ball for a tail. Attach tail in the same manner as ears. Form 2 tablespoons of popcorn into shoe shapes for each foot and press in front of the mound or "body." To form arms, shape a tablespoon of popcorn into a crescent for each arm. Press these shapes into the sides of the body. Tie a ribbon around the rabbit's neck and insert 3 toothpicks on each side of the face for whiskers. Set in an Easter basket or wrap in colored cellophane.

Preparation Time: 15 minutes
Assembling Time: 15 minutes

Over 250 calories
Over 40 grams carbohydrate

CARAMEL EASTER CHARACTERS

Makes 6 to 8 Characters

1 tablespoon oil
½ cup liquid barley malt
½ cup non-instant skim milk
  powder

Heat oil over medium heat in a cast-iron frying pan. Stir in malt and milk powder. Cook, stirring constantly, for 5 minutes until mixture reaches soft-ball stage. (The longer this mixture is cooked the harder the candy will be.) Remove from heat. When mixture is cooled just enough to handle comfortably, moisten hands with water, and press into oiled Easter character molds. When fully cooled remove from molds. If candy does not come out of mold easily, place mold into warm water, making sure that no water enters the mold. When candy softens slightly it can be more easily removed.

Preparation Time: 15 minutes
Assembling Time: 15 minutes

Approximately 225 calories per serving
Over 35 grams carbohydrate per serving

CHEWY CASHEW EGGS

Makes 20 Candies

⅓ cup light cream
½ cup liquid barley malt
1 cup chopped cashews

In a saucepan, combine cream and malt. Cook over medium heat until mixture boils. Continue boiling until soft-ball stage is reached. Remove from heat and cool just until mixture can be easily handled. With moistened hands, shape into small eggs and roll in cashews while still warm.

Preparation Time: 30 minutes
Assembling Time: 10 minutes

Under 150 calories per candy
(Malt is a concentrated, high-carbohydrate food)

ALMOND COCONUT CREAM EGGS
Makes 16 to 20 Eggs

½ cup soft cream cheese
¼ cup frozen apple juice concentrate, thawed
1 cup unsweetened shredded
   coconut
¼ teaspoon almond extract
3–4 tablespoons non-instant
   skim milk powder

Cream all ingredients to form a moldable dough. With moistened hands, form into egg shapes. Cover and refrigerate overnight until firm. These candies should be refrigerated between servings.

Preparation Time: 5 minutes
Assembling Time: 15 minutes

Under 150 calories per serving
Approximately 30 grams carbohydrate per serving

PASTEL PUNCH
Serves 6 to 8

3 cups pineapple juice
1 cup frozen unsweetened
   melon balls

Pour juice into cups and place 3 melon balls in each cup.

Preparation Time: 10 minutes

Under 150 calories per serving
Under 30 grams carbohydrate per serving

7

Midsummer Fresh Fruit Desserts for the Fourth of July

PERSIMMON SHERBET

Serves 6

6 persimmons

Cut persimmons in half. Place a piece of wax paper over cut edge and freeze for 2 hours. Allow to thaw for 15 minutes before serving

Freezing Time: 2 hours
Thawing Time: 15 minutes

Under 150 calories per serving
Approximately 20 grams carbohydrate per serving

EASY BANANA SHERBET WITH HOT CAROB SAUCE

Serves 6

4 ripe bananas
½ cup water
¾ cup roasted carob powder
1 tablespoon butter
1 tablespoon pineapple juice

Peel bananas, wrap in wax paper and freeze. Remove from freezer and thaw slightly while making carob sauce. Combine water, carob powder and butter in a saucepan. Heat, stirring occasionally, for 10 minutes until thickened. Reduce heat to low. Purée bananas and pineapple juice in an electric blender, food processor or juicer until smooth. Spoon into dessert dishes and serve with hot sauce.

Freezing Time: 2 to 3 hours
Preparation Time: 15 minutes

Under 150 calories per serving
Approximately 20 grams carbohydrate per serving

SIMPLE AVOCADO SHERBET *with Pineapple Sauce*   *Serves 6 to 8*

4 avocados
2 tablespoons frozen pineapple
   juice concentrate, thawed
1 16-ounce crushed pineapple
1 tablespoon cornstarch

Freezing Time: 2 to 3 hours
Preparation Time: 15 minutes

Mash ripe avocados with pineapple juice concentrate. Cover and refrigerate until frozen. Remove from freezer and thaw for 10 minutes while making sauce.

   Heat pineapple in its juice with cornstarch mixed in until thickened. Remove from heat. Purée avocado mixture in an electric blender or food processor until smooth. Spoon into dessert dishes and top with sauce.

Under 150 calories per serving
Under 30 grams carbohydrate per serving

SHERBET-STUFFED MELONS   *Serves 8*

2 cups apple juice
6 ounces frozen pineapple juice
   concentrate, thawed
2 ripe bananas
4 melons
3 tablespoons unsweetened
   shredded coconut

Freezing Time: 3 hours
Preparation Time: 15 minutes

In an electric blender, purée apple juice, pineapple juice concentrate and bananas until smooth. Pour into a covered plastic container and freeze for 1 hour until firm at edges. Remove from freezer and beat until smooth. Cover and place back in freezer for 2 hours. Remove from freezer and thaw for 15 minutes before serving. Cut melons in half and remove seeds and pulp. Scoop sherbet into cavities and sprinkle with coconut.

Under 150 calories per serving
Over 30 grams carbohydrate per serving

STRAWBERRY ICE CREAM PARFAITS

Serves 8

ICE CREAM INGREDIENTS
1 tablespoon unflavored gelatin
½ cup boiling apple juice
3 cups crushed fresh strawberries
1 cup heavy cream, whipped

SAUCE INGREDIENTS
2 cups fresh strawberries
½ cup apple juice

Preparation Time: 15 minutes
Freezing Time: 2 hours
Assembling Time: 10 minutes

Dissolve gelatin in boiling apple juice. Let cool. Stir in crushed strawberries. Fold in cream. Place in a covered plastic container and freeze for 1 hour. Process in an ice cream maker and serve directly or chill until firm.

To make sauce, combine strawberries and apple juice and mash with a potato masher. To make parfaits, alternate layers of ice cream and strawberries in parfait glasses.

Approximately 225 calories per serving
Approximately 30 grams carbohydrate per serving

JELLED SHERRIED FRUIT

Serves 8

2 envelopes unflavored gelatin
3½ cups apricot nectar
2 peaches, peeled, pitted and sliced
1 cantaloupe, in balls
½ cup fresh strawberries, halved
½ cup unsweetened shredded coconut
½ cup sherry

Preparation Time: 15 minutes
Chilling Time: 3 hours

In a saucepan, sprinkle gelatin over apricot nectar and heat until gelatin is dissolved. Remove from heat and cool. Stir in remaining ingredients. Chill in a gelatin mold for 3 hours until firm. Unmold to serve.

Under 150 calories per serving
Over 30 grams carbohydrate per serving

GRAPE MOUSSE

Serves 8

2 envelopes unflavored gelatin
3 cups white grape juice
2 cups seedless green grapes
1 teaspoon vanilla
3 egg whites
½ cup heavy cream
Small green grape clusters, for
  garnish

Preparation Time: 20 minutes
Chilling Time: 4 hours

Sprinkle gelatin over grape juice and heat in a sauce-pan until dissolved. Remove from heat and cool. Stir in grapes and vanilla. Chill until mixture has consistency of custard, but is not set, about 1 hour. Beat egg whites until stiff and glossy. Fold into chilled gelatin mixture. Beat cream and fold in. Pour into an 8-cup gelatin mold and chill until firm, about 3 hours. Un-mold and set on a plate garnished with grape clusters.

Under 150 calories per serving
Approximately 30 grams carbohydrate per serving

PASTEL PARFAITS

Serves 10

HONEYDEW MOUSSE INGRE-
DIENTS
2 envelopes unflavored gelatin
¼ cup frozen apple juice concentrate, thawed
1 cup milk
1½ tablespoons cornstarch or
  arrowroot starch dissolved in
  1 tablespoon apple juice
1 honeydew melon, seeded,
  peeled and cut up
3 egg whites

To prepare honeydew mousse, combine gelatin and apple juice concentrate and set aside. In a saucepan, heat milk nearly to boiling. Stir in cornstarch paste and continue to cook, stirring occasionally, until thick-ened. Remove from heat and immediately stir in gela-tin mixture. In a blender or food processor, blend melon until smooth. Stir into gelatin and milk mixture. Chill for 1 hour until mixture is consistency of custard but not set. Beat egg whites until stiff and fold into jelled mixture. Return to refrigerator while preparing cantaloupe mousse in the same way, substituting can-taloupe purée for honeydew purée. Alternate layers in parfait glasses and chill for 1 hour before serving.

CANTALOUPE MOUSSE

INGREDIENTS

2 envelopes unflavored gelatin

¼ cup frozen apple juice concentrate, thawed

1 cup milk

1½ tablespoons cornstarch or
arrowroot starch dissolved in
1 tablespoon apple juice

1 cantaloupe, seeded, peeled
and cut up

3 egg whites

Preparation Time: 25 minutes
Chilling Time: 4 hours

Under 150 calories per serving
Approximately 30 grams carbohydrate per serving

STRAWBERRY CHIFFON PIE

Serves 8

½ Flaky Pie Dough recipe (see
p. 16)

1 envelope unflavored gelatin

¼ cup apple juice

1 cup milk

1½ tablespoons cornstarch or
arrowroot starch mixed with
1 tablespoon frozen apple
juice concentrate, thawed

1½ cups mashed fresh strawberries

3 egg whites

Preparation Time: 25 minutes
Chilling Time: 3 hours

Preheat oven to 350 degrees. Prepare dough and line a 9-inch pie plate. Bake for 20 minutes until golden brown.

Sprinkle gelatin over apple juice and set aside. In a saucepan, heat milk nearly to boiling. Stir in cornstarch paste and continue to cook, stirring constantly, until mixture thickens. Remove from heat and immediately stir in mashed strawberries. Chill mixture for 1 hour until it resembles the texture of custard but is not set, about 40 minutes.

Beat egg whites until stiff and glossy. Fold into jelled mixture. Pour into pie shell and chill for 2 hours until set.

Under 150 calories per serving
Approximately 20 grams carbohydrate per serving

GLAZED BLUEBERRY PIE

Serves 8

½ Flaky Pastry Dough recipe
  (see p. 16)
3 tablespoons cornstarch
⅔ cup blueberries
½ cup water
1 tablespoon frozen apple juice
  concentrate, thawed
1 quart blueberries

Preparation Time: 20 minutes
Chilling Time: 2 hours

Preheat oven to 350 degrees. Prepare dough and line a 9-inch pie plate. Bake for 20 minutes until golden brown. In an electric blender or food processor, blend cornstarch, ⅔ cup blueberries, water and apple juice concentrate. In a saucepan, heat mixture over medium heat, stirring occasionally, until thickened. Remove from heat and stir in blueberries. Pour into baked pie shell and chill for 2 hours until set.

Under 150 calories per serving
Approximately 30 grams carbohydrate per serving

GLAZED PEACH PIE

Serves 8

½ Flaky Pastry Dough recipe
  (see p. 16)
3 tablespoons cornstarch
½ cup peeled, diced peaches
½ cup apple juice
2 tablespoons frozen apple
  juice concentrate, thawed
4 cups peeled, sliced peaches

Preparation Time: 20 minutes
Chilling Time: 2 hours

Preheat oven to 350 degrees. Prepare dough and line a 9-inch pie plate. Bake for 20 minutes until golden brown.

In an electric blender or food processor, blend cornstarch, peaches, apple juice and apple juice concentrate. In a saucepan, heat mixture, stirring occasionally, until thickened. Fold in peaches and pour into baked pie shell. Chill for 2 hours until set.

Under 150 calories per serving
Approximately 30 grams carbohydrate per serving

WATERMELON GELATIN

Serves 8

2 cups watermelon, in chunks
  with seeds removed
1½ cups strawberries
2 envelopes unflavored gelatin
½ cup apple juice

Preparation Time: 10 minutes
Chilling Time: 3 hours

In an electric blender, liquefy watermelon and strawberries, and set aside. In a saucepan, heat gelatin and apple juice until gelatin dissolves. Stir into liquefied fruit. Pour into a 4-cup gelatin mold and chill for 3 hours until firm. Unmold to serve.

Under 150 calories per serving
Approximately 30 grams carbohydrate per serving

STRAWBERRY CREAM GELATIN

Serves 8

2 envelopes unflavored gelatin
1½ cups white grape juice
3 cups sliced strawberries
⅔ cup cream cheese or part-
  skim milk ricotta
½ cup milk

Preparation Time: 15 minutes
Chilling Time: 4 hours

In a saucepan, combine gelatin and grape juice. Heat until gelatin is dissolved. Remove from heat and cool. Stir in 2 cups sliced strawberries and set aside. In an electric blender, blend remaining strawberries, cream cheese or ricotta and milk until smooth. Fold into gelatin mixture. Pour into a 6-cup gelatin mold and chill for 4 hours until set. Unmold to serve.

Approximately 225 calories per serving
Approximately 30 grams carbohydrate per serving

FRESH PEACH SOUFFLÉ

Serves 8 to 10

2 cups peeled, sliced peaches
3 tablespoons frozen apple
  juice concentrate, thawed
3 tablespoons unsalted soft butter

Preheat oven to 350 degrees. Toss 1½ cups peaches with apple juice concentrate and set remaining ½ cup peaches aside for later use. Line the bottom of a buttered 2-quart soufflé dish with peach-and-apple-juice mixture.

3 tablespoons brown rice flour
⅔ cup milk
4 eggs, separated
1 tablespoon frozen pineapple
    juice concentrate, thawed

In a saucepan, melt butter and stir in flour to form a paste. Gradually add milk, stirring constantly until mixture begins to thicken. Beat in egg yolks and continue to cook until thickened. Remove from heat and cool. Beat egg whites until firm and glossy. Fold into thickened mixture. In a blender, purée remaining ½ cup peaches and pineapple juice concentrate. Fold purée into soufflé batter. Pour into soufflé dish and bake for 40 to 45 minutes until golden and fluffy.

Preparation Time: 20 minutes
Baking Time: 40 to 45 minutes

Under 150 calories per serving
Approximately 20 grams carbohydrate per serving

PEACHES AND CREAM CAKE

Serves 9

2 cups whole wheat pastry flour
½ teaspoon baking powder
⅓ cup unsalted soft butter
9 fresh peach halves, peeled
    and pitted
2 teaspoons cinnamon
¼ cup apple juice concentrate

1 egg yolk
1 cup light cream

Preheat oven to 375 degrees. In a bowl, mix flour and baking powder. Work butter into flour with fingers until mixture resembles a coarse meal. Spread half mixture over the bottom of an oiled 9-inch square baking dish. Top with peach halves, distributed in 3 rows of 3. Sprinkle remaining flour mixture over peaches. Combine cinnamon and apple juice concentrate and pour over cake. Bake for 20 minutes. Beat together egg yolk and cream and pour over partially baked cake. Bake another 10 to 15 minutes until done. Serve while hot.

Preparation Time: 15 minutes
Baking Time: 30 to 40 minutes

Approximately 225 calories per serving
Over 35 grams carbohydrate per serving

STRAWBERRY SHORTCAKE

Serves 6

BISCUIT INGREDIENTS
1 cup whole wheat pastry flour
2 teaspoons baking powder
2 tablespoons oil
⅓ cup milk
2 teaspoons frozen apple juice
   concentrate, thawed

TOPPING INGREDIENTS
4 cups sliced, mashed fresh
   strawberries
3 tablespoons frozen apple
   juice concentrate, thawed
1 cup heavy cream, whipped,
   or 1 cup part-skim milk ricotta cheese blended with 1
   tablespoon apple juice concentrate

Preheat oven to 400 degrees. In a bowl, mix flour and baking powder with a wire whisk. With a fork or pastry blender work in oil until mixture resembles a coarse meal. Stir in milk and apple juice concentrate to form a biscuit dough. Roll dough and cut into 2-inch circles with a cookie cutter. Place on a well-oiled baking sheet and bake for 15 minutes until lightly browned. Remove from oven and set aside.

To make strawberry topping, stir together strawberries and apple juice concentrate. Split biscuits and top with strawberry mixture. Top with whipped cream or ricotta before serving.

Preparation and Baking Time: 30 minutes

Approximately 225 calories per serving
Approximately 30 grams carbohydrate per serving

FRESH BAKED PEACHES

Serves 12

6 peaches, peeled, halved and
   pitted
4 tablespoons currants
4 tablespoons unsweetened
   shredded coconut

Preheat oven to 350 degrees. Prepare peach halves and set them with cavities facing up in a covered baking dish. In a bowl, combine currants, coconut, almonds and pineapple juice concentrate. Place 1 tablespoon of mixture into the cavity of each peach half.

4 tablespoons chopped almonds
2 tablespoons frozen pineapple
  juice concentrate, thawed
3 tablespoons water

Preparation Time: 10 minutes
Baking Time: 20 minutes

Pour water into the bottom of the dish, cover and bake for 20 minutes until peaches are tender.

Approximately 150 calories per serving
Approximately 30 grams carbohydrate per serving

STRAWBERRIES ROMANOFF   *Serves 8*

1 envelope unflavored gelatin
⅓ cup fresh orange juice
3 cups sliced strawberries
3 tablespoons frozen apple
  juice concentrate, thawed
2 tablespoons grated orange
  peel
1 cup heavy cream, whipped,
  or 1½ cups part-skim milk ricotta cheese blended with 1
  tablespoon frozen apple juice
  concentrate, thawed

Sprinkle gelatin over orange juice and heat until dissolved. Stir in strawberries, apple juice concentrate and grated orange peel. Cool. Fold in whipped cream or ricotta. Pour into a 1-quart gelatin mold and chill for 3 hours. Unmold and serve.

Preparation Time: 15 minutes
Chilling Time: 3 hours

Approximately 225 calories per serving
Approximately 30 grams carbohydrate per serving

BERRY ZABAGLIONE

Serves 8

1 quart fresh berries (whole strawberries, blueberries or raspberries)
2 egg yolks
1 tablespoon cornstarch
¾ cup cream sherry

Preparation Time: 5 minutes
Cooking Time: 5 minutes

Place ½ cup berries in 8 stemware glasses. In a saucepan, combine egg yolks, cornstarch and sherry. Heat without boiling, stirring constantly, until mixture thickens. Spoon 2 tablespoons of sauce over each serving of berries

Under 150 calories per serving
Approximately 30 grams carbohydrate per serving

STRAWBERRY CAKE

Serves 12

CAKE INGREDIENTS
½ cup oil
5 eggs, separated
⅓ cup liquid barley malt
1⅓ cups strawberry-apple juice
1⅓ cups whole wheat pastry flour
1⅓ cups brown rice flour
⅓ cup non-instant skim milk powder
1 tablespoon baking powder

2 teaspoons almond extract

FROSTING INGREDIENTS
¼ cup soft butter
1½ cups non-instant skim milk powder
½ cup fresh sliced strawberries

Preheat oven to 350 degrees. To make cake, beat oil, egg yolks, malt and strawberry juice. In a separate bowl, combine whole wheat pastry flour, brown rice flour, milk powder and baking powder and stir with a wire whisk. Gradually add flour mixture to liquid to form a smooth batter. Beat egg whites and almond extract until stiff and fold into batter. Pour into 2 well-oiled and dusted cake pans or a 10-inch oiled springform pan. Bake for 1½ hours or until a toothpick comes out clean when inserted into the center of cake. Cool for 10 minutes, remove from pans and cool on a wire rack.

To make frosting, blend butter, milk powder, sliced strawberries and apple juice concentrate in an electric blender or food processor until smooth. If using a springform pan, cut into two layers. Frost the bottom layer, cover with the top layer, frost the rest of the cake and decorate with fresh strawberry halves.

2 tablespoons frozen apple
juice concentrate, thawed
10 whole strawberries, halved

Preparation Time: 20 minutes
Baking Time: 1½ hours
Assembling Time: 15 minutes

This cake can be served at a summer party or placed in a decorative tin and given as a summer surprise.

Approximately 225 calories per serving
Over 35 grams carbohydrate per serving

STRAWBERRY TURNOVERS
Serves 8

Flaky Pastry Dough or Stretchy
Pastry Dough recipe (see p.
16)
3 cups sliced strawberries
2 tablespoons frozen apple
juice concentrate, thawed
1 teaspoon vanilla
3 tablespoons cornstarch or arrowroot starch
1 egg yolk, beaten

Preparation Time: 20 minutes
Baking Time: 30 minutes

Preheat oven to 350 degrees. Roll dough into a rectangle and cut into 8 squares. In a bowl, mix strawberries, apple juice concentrate, vanilla and cornstarch. Spoon equal portions of filling onto each square. Fold pastry over filling to form triangles. Place on an oiled baking sheet, brush with egg yolk and bake for 30 minutes until golden brown.

Placed in a decorative tin, these turnovers make a welcome summer hostess gift.

Approximately 150 calories per serving
Approximately 30 grams carbohydrate per serving

STRAWBERRY RICOTTA PIE

Serves 8

½ Flaky Pastry Dough recipe
  (see p. 16)
¾ cup part-skim milk ricotta
  cheese
¼ cup milk
3 eggs, separated
1 teaspoon vanilla
1 tablespoon soy flour
3 tablespoons frozen apple
  juice concentrate, thawed
2 cups sliced strawberries
2 tablespoons cornstarch

Preparation Time: 20 minutes
Baking Time: 45 minutes

Preheat oven to 400 degrees. Prepare dough, line a 9-inch pie plate and bake for 10 minutes.

In a blender, purée ricotta, milk, egg yolks, vanilla, soy flour and apple juice concentrate. In a bowl, toss strawberries with cornstarch until thoroughly coated. Fold strawberries into ricotta mixture. Beat egg whites until stiff and fold in. Pour into partially baked pie shell. Bake for 30 minutes until set and just lightly golden at tips. Cool before serving.

Placed in a round decorative tin, this fancy pie can be a delicious gift.

Approximately 150 calories per serving
Approximately 20 grams carbohydrate per serving

RASPBERRY CREAM PIE

Serves 8

½ Flaky Pastry Dough recipe
  (see p. 16)
2 cups milk
1 teaspoon vanilla
⅓ cup brown rice flour
2 tablespoons frozen apple
  juice concentrate, thawed
3 egg yolks
2 cups raspberries

Preheat oven to 350 degrees. Line pie plate with crust. Bake for 15 to 20 minutes until lightly browned. Remove from oven and cool.

In a saucepan, combine milk, vanilla, brown rice flour, apple juice concentrate, egg yolks and ½ cup raspberries. Cook without boiling, stirring occasionally, until mixture thickens to custard consistency. Pour into pie shell.

In a separate saucepan, combine blended raspberries and cornstarch or arrowroot starch. Cook, stirring constantly, until mixture is thick. Remove from heat

⅓ cup raspberries blended with
  ⅓ cup white grape juice until
  smooth
1 tablespoon cornstarch or arrowroot starch

and fold in remaining 1½ cups raspberries. Spread raspberry mixture over custard mixture. Cool before serving.

This pie serves as a welcome gift for a summertime party or Fourth of July picnic.

Preparation and Cooking Time:
30 minutes

Approximately 150 calories per serving
Approximately 30 grams carbohydrate per serving

STRAWBERRY STRUDEL

Serves 10 to 12

¼ Strudel recipe (see p. 17)
2½ cups sliced strawberries
2 tablespoons frozen apple
  juice concentrate, thawed
3 tablespoons cornstarch or arrowroot starch

Preheat oven to 350 degrees. Prepare strudel dough.

In a bowl, toss strawberries with apple juice concentrate and cornstarch until well coated. Place on rolled-out strudel dough and roll according to directions on p. 17. Place on an oiled and flour-dusted baking sheet and bake for 40 minutes until lightly browned and crisp.

This strudel recipe can also be made with fresh peaches, blueberries or raspberries.

It can be eaten as a summer treat or wrapped in red cellophane and decorated with a blue bow as a July Fourth gift.

Preparation Time: 30 minutes
Baking Time: 40 minutes

Approximately 225 calories per serving
Approximately 30 grams carbohydrate per serving

BLUEBERRY BREAD

Serves 15 to 20

BREAD BATTER INGREDIENTS
¼ cup oil
1 cup orange juice
3 eggs
1 tablespoon grated orange peel
¼ cup liquid barley malt
2 teaspoons baking soda
1 cup whole wheat pastry flour
¾ cup brown rice flour
¼ cup non-instant skim milk powder
1¼ cups fresh blueberries
1 tablespoon arrowroot or cornstarch

FROSTING INGREDIENTS
2 tablespoons soft butter
⅔ cup non-instant skim milk powder
¼ cup pineapple or orange juice

Preparation Time: 15 minutes
Baking Time: 1 hour

Preheat oven to 350 degrees.

In a bowl, beat oil, orange juice, eggs, orange peel and liquid barley malt. In a separate bowl, mix baking soda, pastry flour, rice flour and milk powder with a wire whisk. Gradually mix dry mixture into liquids to form a smooth batter. Add blueberries tossed with cornstarch. Pour into a well-oiled loaf pan and bake for 1 hour until a toothpick inserted into the center comes out clean. Cool for 10 minutes and remove from pan, then cool on a wire rack.

To make frosting, blend soft butter, milk powder and juice in an electric blender or food processor until smooth. Spread frosting over loaf so that it drips over sides. Allow to stand a half-hour so frosting can set.

Place in a decorative loaf tin and use as a hostess gift.

Approximately 150 calories per serving
Over 35 grams carbohydrate per serving

FRESH FRUIT AND CUSTARD ROLL

Serves 9

CAKE INGREDIENTS
1 large ripe banana
3 eggs, separated
2 tablespoons whole wheat
  pastry flour
2 tablespoons brown rice flour
½ teaspoon baking powder
1 tablespoon liquid barley malt
1 teaspoon almond extract

FILLING INGREDIENTS
2 cups milk
3 tablespoons cornstarch
1 teaspoon cinnamon or cardamom
4 egg yolks
2 tablespoons frozen apple
  juice concentrate, thawed
1 cup finely chopped and
  drained fresh fruit (peaches,
  strawberries, or apricots)

ASSEMBLING INGREDIENTS
⅓ cup unsweetened shredded
  coconut
⅓ cup finely ground almonds

Preparation Time: 30 minutes
Baking Time: 15 minutes
Assembling Time: 45 minutes

To make jelly roll cake, blend banana and 3 egg yolks in an electric blender or food processor until smooth. In a bowl, combine pastry flour, rice flour and baking powder, stirring with a wire whisk. Add dry ingredients to banana and egg mixture. Stir in barley malt and almond extract. Beat 3 egg whites until stiff and fold into batter.

Preheat oven to 375 degrees. Oil a 9 x 13-inch jelly roll pan and line it with wax paper and grease paper. Pour batter into prepared pan and bake for 15 minutes.

While cake bakes, prepare filling. In a saucepan, combine milk, cornstarch, cinnamon or cardamom, egg yolks and apple juice concentrate. Heat without boiling, stirring occasionally, until mixture is the consistency of a thick custard. Remove from heat. Cool to lukewarm and stir in fruit.

Sprinkle a clean kitchen towel with coconut and ground almonds. Remove cake from oven and turn onto towel. Carefully remove wax paper. Cut hard edges off cake for easy rolling. Roll in towel and allow to cool. Unroll and spread with custard and fruit mixture. Roll again and place on a serving dish seam side down.

This roll can be cut in 1-inch slices and placed in a decorative tin to be given as a summertime hostess gift.

Approximately 225 calories per serving
Over 35 grams carbohydrate per serving

BLUEBERRY CUPCAKES   *Serves 24*

CUPCAKE INGREDIENTS

⅓ cup oil
5 eggs, separated
½ cup liquid barley malt
1 cup apple juice
1¼ cups whole wheat pastry
    flour
1¼ cups brown rice flour
½ cup non-instant skim milk
    powder
1 tablespoon baking powder
1½ cups blueberries
2 tablespoons cornstarch
1 teaspoon almond extract

FROSTING INGREDIENTS

¼ cup soft butter
1½ cup non-instant milk pow-
    der
½ cup pineapple juice
½ teaspoon almond extract

Preparation Time: 25 minutes
Baking Time: 25 minutes

Preheat oven to 375 degrees. In a bowl, mix oil, egg yolks, malt and apple juice. In a separate bowl, combine pastry flour, brown rice flour, milk powder and baking powder, mixing with a wire whisk. Gradually mix dry ingredients into liquids to form a smooth batter. Toss blueberries with starch and fold into batter. Add almond extract to egg whites and beat until stiff. Fold into batter. Spoon batter into lined cupcake tins and bake for 25 minutes until a toothpick inserted into the center of a cupcake comes out clean.

To make frosting, blend butter, milk powder, pineapple juice and almond extract until smooth and thick in an electric blender or food processor. Frost cupcakes when cooled.

Placed in decorative containers, these cupcakes make a delicious summertime gift.

Approximately 225 calories per serving
Over 35 grams carbohydrate per serving

PEACH COCONUT CUPCAKES   *Serves 24*

CUPCAKE INGREDIENTS
⅓ cup oil

5 eggs, separated

1 cup peach juice

½ cup liquid barley malt

1⅓ cups whole wheat pastry
  flour

1¼ cups brown rice flour

3 tablespoons gluten flour

1 tablespoon baking powder

1 teaspoon almond extract

1 cup peeled, chopped peaches

1 teaspoon cornstarch or arrowroot starch

⅔ cup unsweetened shredded
  coconut

FROSTING INGREDIENTS
¼ cup soft butter

1¼ cups non-instant skim milk
  powder

½ cup unsweetened shredded
  coconut

½ cup apricot juice or peach
  juice

Preparation Time: 25 minutes
Baking Time: 25 minutes

Preheat oven to 375 degrees. In a bowl, mix oil, egg yolks, peach juice and malt. In a separate bowl, mix pastry flour, rice flour, gluten flour and baking powder with a wire whisk. Gradually stir dry mixture into liquids to form a smooth batter. Beat egg whites and almond extract until stiff and fold into batter. Toss peaches with starch and gently fold in peaches and coconut. Spoon batter into lined muffin tins and bake for 25 minutes until golden and a toothpick inserted into the center of a cupcake comes out clean.

To make frosting, blend butter, milk powder, coconut juice in an electric blender or food processor until smooth and thick. When cupcakes are cool, frost.

Place in a decorative tin for a gift.

Approximately 225 calories per serving
Over 35 grams carbohydrate per serving

PLUMS IN PASTRY

Serves 10

Flaky or Stretchy Pastry Dough
recipe (see p. 16)
10 plums, pitted
10 almonds
1 tablespoon frozen apple juice
concentrate, thawed
1 egg yolk mixed with 1 teaspoon apple juice

Preparation Time: 20 minutes
Baking Time: 15 to 20 minutes

Preheat oven to 400 degrees. Prepare pie crust dough and roll out. Cut into circles large enough to wrap around plums and gather at the top. Insert one almond into the cavity of each plum and drip in a small amount of apple juice concentrate. Wrap plums in pastry, gathering circles at the top but leaving a small opening for steam to escape. Place on a well-oiled baking sheet and brush with egg and apple juice mixture. Bake for 15 to 20 minutes until pastry is golden brown.

These delicate plum pastries make a lovely gift when placed in a decorative container.

Under 150 calories per serving
Approximately 20 grams carbohydrate per serving

GLAZED STRAWBERRY TARTS

Serves 12

Stretchy Pastry Dough or Flaky
Pastry Dough recipe (see p.
16)
3 tablespoons cornstarch or arrowroot starch
⅔ cup sliced strawberries
⅔ cup apple juice
3 cups fresh whole strawberries

Preheat oven to 400 degrees. Roll out pie dough and cut into 12 3⅓-inch circles. Turn a muffin tin upside down. Oil the backs of each tin and form the circles of dough over each tin. Bake for 10 to 15 minutes until tart shells are lightly browned and firm. Remove from oven and cool while preparing filling.

In an electric blender or food processor, blend cornstarch, sliced strawberries and apple juice until smooth. Turn into a saucepan, and heat until thickened. Remove from heat and stir in whole strawberries. Remove tart shells from muffin tins and spoon filling into shells.

These pretty red tarts can be arranged in a decorative tin and used as a hostess gift at summertime parties or picnics.

Preparation Time: 30 minutes
Baking Time: 15 minutes

Approximately 150 calories per serving
Approximately 20 grams carbohydrate per serving

FRESH FRUIT LOGS

Serves 15

DOUGH INGREDIENTS

1 cup warm apple juice
1 tablespoon baking yeast
3 tablespoons melted butter
3 tablespoons frozen apple juice concentrate, thawed
2 eggs, beaten
2¼ cups whole wheat pastry flour
¾ cup soy flour
¾ cup gluten flour

FILLING INGREDIENTS

2 cups fresh, peeled, chopped peaches, sliced strawberries and/or blueberries
2 tablespoons cornstarch or arrowroot starch
1 tablespoon frozen apple juice concentrate, thawed
1 teaspoon grated lemon peel

To make dough, place warm apple juice in a bowl. Sprinkle yeast over juice. Allow to stand until yeast dissolves. Stir in melted butter, apple juice concentrate and eggs. In a separate bowl, mix pastry flour, soy flour and gluten flour with a wire whisk. Beat 1¾ cups of flour mixture into liquids. Cover and let stand for 30 minutes until sponge forms. Beat in remaining flour mixture, turn onto a well-floured board and knead until smooth and elastic. If dough becomes sticky, knead in additional pastry flour. Oil dough and place in a bowl. Cover with a damp, warm towel and set in a warm place to rise for 1½ hours.

While dough rises, prepare filling. Place fresh fruit, cornstarch, apple juice concentrate and grated lemon peel in a bowl and stir until well distributed. When dough has risen, roll into a 15 x 16-inch rectangle, brush with melted butter and spread fruit mixture evenly over rectangle. Roll in jelly roll fashion along the 15-inch edge. Cut into 3 5-inch logs. Seal seams. Cover and let rise until doubled in bulk, about 1 hour. Preheat oven to 400 degrees. Bake for 25 to 30 minutes on a well-oiled baking sheet. Cool.

FROSTING INGREDIENTS
¼ cup soft unsalted butter
1¼ cups non-instant skim milk
  powder
1 teaspoon almond extract
½ cup peeled, sliced peaches or
  sliced strawberries
2 tablespoons frozen apple
  juice concentrate, thawed

Preparation Time: 3 to 4 hours
Baking Time: 25 to 30 minutes

To make frosting, blend butter, milk powder, almond extract, fruit and apple juice concentrate in an electric blender or food processor until smooth. Drizzle frosting over rolls.

These can be served warm or packed in decorative tins as a summertime gift.

Approximately 225 calories per serving
Over 35 grams carbohydrate per serving

SUMMER EGGNOG

Serves 10 to 12

4 cups milk
3 eggs, separated
1 teaspoon almond extract
2 tablespoons frozen pineapple
  juice concentrate, thawed
1 cup fresh strawberries,
  chopped peaches or melon

Preparation Time: 10 minutes

In an electric blender or food processor, blend milk, egg yolks, almond extract, pineapple juice concentrate and fruit until smooth. Beat whites until stiff and fold into fruit eggnog.

Approximately 150 calories per serving
Approximately 30 grams carbohydrate per serving

COLD CAROB
Serves 6 to 8

¼ cup roasted carob powder
⅓ cup warm water
1 teaspoon vanilla
1 quart milk
8 ice cubes

Preparation Time: 5 minutes

Combine carob powder and water in a blender. Add vanilla, milk and ice cubes. Blend for 3 minutes until ice cubes are chopped and drink is foamy. Serve in tall glasses.

Under 150 calories per serving
Approximately 20 grams carbohydrate per serving

COLD MOCHA
Serves 6 to 8

2 tablespoons roasted carob powder
2 tablespoons grain coffee substitute
2 teaspoons vanilla
1 cup hot water
3 tablespoons non-instant skim milk powder
3 cups milk
8 ice cubes

Preparation Time: 5 minutes

In an electric blender, combine carob powder, grain coffee substitute, vanilla and hot water. Add milk powder, milk and ice cubes and blend until ice is chopped. Pour into tall glasses to serve.

Under 150 calories per serving
Approximately 20 grams carbohydrate per serving

SPARKLING PINK PUNCH

Serves 12 to 16

1 quart strawberry-apple juice
2 cups cold Red Zinger tea
1 quart mineral water
2 cups whole frozen strawberries

Preparation Time: 5 minutes

In a punch bowl, combine juice, tea and mineral water. Add frozen strawberries before serving.

Under 150 calories per serving
Under 20 grams carbohydrate per serving

PIÑA-COLADA PUNCH

Serves 12 to 16

1 16-ounce can unsweetened
pineapple rings
1 quart pineapple juice
1 quart coconut juice

Preparation Time: 5 minutes

Remove pineapple rings from can and freeze on a baking sheet. In a punch bowl, combine pineapple juice and coconut juice. Place frozen pineapple rings in punch as a float.

Approximately 150 calories per serving
Approximately 30 grams carbohydrate per serving

Children's July Fourth Treats

RED, WHITE AND BLUE PIE

Serves 8

½ Flaky Pie dough recipe (see
p. 16)

CUSTARD FILLING
INGREDIENTS

Preheat oven to 350 degrees. Roll dough and line a 9-inch pie plate. Bake for 20 minutes until golden.

To make custard filling, combine milk, egg yolks, apple juice concentrate, and cornstarch in a saucepan.

2 cups milk
4 egg yolks
2 tablespoons frozen apple
  juice concentrate, thawed
3 tablespoons cornstarch
1 teaspoon vanilla

RED TOPPING INGREDIENTS
⅔ cup strawberries puréed with
  ½ cup apple juice
2 tablespoons cornstarch
1½ cups sliced fresh strawberries

BLUE TOPPING INGREDIENTS
⅔ cup blueberries puréed with
  ½ cup apple juice
2 tablespoons cornstarch
1½ cups blueberries

STAR INGREDIENTS
1 tablespoon soft unsalted butter
¼ cup non-instant skim milk
  powder
1 tablespoon frozen apple juice
  concentrate, thawed

Preparation and Cooking Time:
30 minutes

Heat without boiling, stirring occasionally, until mixture thickens to a custard. Remove from heat and stir in vanilla. Pour into baked pie shell and cool.

To prepare red topping, combine strawberry and apple juice purée with cornstarch in a saucepan and heat until thick. Stir in sliced stawberries. Set aside.

To prepare blue topping, combine blueberry and apple juice purée with starch in a saucepan. Heat until thick, remove from heat and stir in blueberries. Set aside.

To make frosting for stars, blend butter, milk powder and apple juice concentrate in an electric blender or food processor until smooth and thick. To decorate pie, alternate red and blue toppings in 8 wedge pie shapes over custard layer to mark 8 serving pieces. Spoon frosting into cake decorating bag and decorate with stars.

Approximately 225 calories per serving
Approximately 30 grams carbohydrate per serving

FLAG CAKE

Serves 12

CAKE INGREDIENTS
½ cup oil
5 eggs, separated
1 cup strawberry juice
½ cup liquid barley malt
1¼ cups whole wheat pastry flour
1⅓ cups brown rice flour
⅓ cup non-instant skim milk powder
1 tablespoon baking powder
1 teaspoon almond extract
1 cup blueberries
2 teaspoons cornstarch

RED FROSTING INGREDIENTS
½ cup strawberries puréed with ⅔ cup apple juice
3 tablespoons cornstarch

BLUE FROSTING INGREDIENTS
½ cup blueberries puréed with ⅔ cup apple juice
3 tablespoons cornstarch

WHITE TOPPING INGREDIENTS
1 cup heavy cream
1 teaspoon vanilla
1 tablespoon frozen apple juice concentrate, thawed

Preheat oven to 350 degrees. To make cake, mix oil, egg yolks, strawberry juice and malt. In a separate bowl, mix pastry flour, rice flour, milk powder and baking powder with a wire whisk until well distributed. Gradually mix dry ingredients into liquid ingredients to form a smooth batter. Beat egg whites and almond extract until stiff, and fold into batter. Toss blueberries with cornstarch until well coated and fold into batter. Pour into a well-oiled and dusted 9 x 12 x 2-inch baking pan. Bake for 1½ hours until a toothpick inserted into the center comes out clean. Cool for 10 minutes, remove from pan and cool completely on a wire rack.

To make red frosting, combine strawberry purée and cornstarch in a saucepan and heat, stirring constantly until thickened. Remove from heat and set aside.

To make blue frosting, combine blueberry purée and starch and heat until thickened, stirring constantly.

To make white topping, whip the heavy cream, vanilla and juice concentrate.

To decorate cake, use 3 colors of frosting to imitate the American flag. In the corner of the cake, make a blue rectangle with the blue frosting. Alternate red and white toppings to make stripes. Leave enough whipped cream to fill a pastry bag and decorate blue area with 50 stars. Garnish the blue area that remains visible with blueberries, and place strawberry halves one next to the other on the red stripes.

GARNISH INGREDIENTS
1½ cups halved strawberries
1½ cups blueberries

Preparation Time: 20 minutes
Baking Time: 90 minutes

Over 250 calories per serving
Over 35 grams carbohydrate per serving

RED, WHITE AND BLUE GELATIN

Serves 12

RED GELATIN INGREDIENTS
1 envelope unflavored gelatin
1¼ cups apple juice
2 cups fresh strawberries

BLUE GELATIN
1 envelope unflavored gelatin
1¼ cups apple juice
2 cups blueberries

WHITE GELATIN
1 envelope unflavored gelatin
1¼ cups apple juice
1 cup part-skim milk ricotta
  cheese
1 teaspoon vanilla

To make red gelatin, combine gelatin and apple juice in a saucepan. Heat over low heat until gelatin dissolves and pour into an electric blender with one cup strawberries. Blend until smooth. Stir in remaining strawberries and pour into a gelatin mold. Chill for 3 hours until firm.

To make blue layer of gelatin, combine gelatin and apple juice in saucepan and heat until gelatin is dissolved. Pour into an electric blender jar with 1 cup of blueberries and blend until smooth. Stir in remaining blueberries. Cool and then pour mixture over firm red layer. Chill until firm.

To make final white layer, combine gelatin and apple juice in a saucepan and heat until gelatin is dissolved. Cool. Place gelatin mixture, ricotta and vanilla in an electric blender and blend until smooth. Pour over firm blue layer and refrigerate until firm. Unmold to serve.

Preparation Time: 20 minutes
Chilling Time: 9 hours

Under 150 calories per serving
Approximately 20 grams carbohydrate per serving

STRIPED POPSICLES

Serves 6 to 8

RED STRIPE INGREDIENTS
¼ cup apple juice
1 cup strawberries

BLUE STRIPE INGREDIENTS
¼ cup apple juice
1 cup blueberries

Preparation Time: 5 minutes
Freezing Time: 6 to 8 hours

In an electric blender, liquefy apple juice and strawberries. Pour into plastic Popsicle makers, filling each half full. Freeze. In a blender, liquefy apple juice and blueberries. Fill Popsicle makers with blueberry mixture. Freeze, once again.

Under 150 calories per serving
Approximately 20 grams carbohydrate per serving

PATRIOTIC SODA

Serves 4 to 6

2 cups purple grape juice
2 cups mineral water
1 cup whole frozen strawberries

Preparation Time: 5 minutes

Combine juice and mineral water. Pour into glasses and place several strawberries in each glass.

Under 150 calories per serving
Approximately 20 grams carbohydrate per serving

8

Fall Fun Foods for Halloween

MERINGUE ORANGES

6 oranges
1½ cups milk
3 tablespoons brown rice flour
2 tablespoons frozen apple
   juice concentrate, thawed
6 eggs, separated
¼ teaspoon cream of tartar
1 teaspoon frozen apple juice
   concentrate, thawed
1 teaspoon orange extract

Slice oranges in half crosswise. To make each orange half stand without support, cut a very thin slice of peel from the bottom. Remove membrane and fruit with a grapefruit knife. Discard membrane and spoon a layer of fruit into each half orange shell. Refrigerate.

In a saucepan, combine milk, rice flour, apple juice concentrate and egg yolks. Heat, stirring occasionally, until mixture thickens to a smooth custard. Spoon 2 tablespoons of custard into each orange shell and return to the refrigerator.

Preheat oven to 400 degrees. In a bowl, beat egg whites and cream of tartar until foamy. Beat in 1 teaspoon apple juice concentrate and orange extract until stiff. Be sure not to underbeat. Pile meringue decoratively on top of oranges, giving the illusion of a whole round shape to each orange. Place meringue-topped oranges on an ungreased baking sheet and bake for several minutes, until meringue tips just turn light brown. Serve immediately.

Preparation Time: 30 minutes
Baking Time: 3 to 4 minutes

Under 150 calories per serving
Approximately 20 grams carbohydrate per serving

SWEET STUFFED PUMPKIN

Serves 12 to 15

2 cups sweet brown rice
3 cups water
4 cups milk
⅔ cup raisins or currants
2 teaspoons ground cardamom
1 teaspoon cinnamon
¼ cup frozen apple juice concentrate, thawed
1 10-pound pumpkin
¼ cup soft unsalted butter
⅔ cup chopped almonds (optional)

In a large pan, combine sweet rice and water. Bring to a boil and reduce heat to low. Cook, covered, for 30 minutes. Stir in milk, raisins or currants, cardamom, cinnamon and apple juice concentrate. Reduce heat to lowest possible temperature and continue to cook for 3 hours.

One hour before rice pudding is fully cooked, prepare pumpkin for stuffing. Preheat oven to 375 degrees. Wash the outside of the pumpkin and cut a lid 7 inches in diameter. Remove lid and stem, but retain for later use as a cover. Clean pulp and seeds from pumpkin. Rub the inside with butter, replace lid and bake for 45 minutes until shell can be pierced with a fork. Spoon rice pudding into pumpkin, cover and bake for a final 15 minutes before serving. Sprinkle with chopped almonds, if desired. Place on a large serving platter, with a ladle so that guests may serve themselves portions of rice pudding and baked pumpkin. This dish is especially conducive to a buffet since it is both a wonderful centerpiece and self-serve food.

Preparation and Baking Time: 4 hours

Approximately 150 calories per serving
Over 35 grams carbohydrate per serving

ORANGE BAVARIAN

Serves 8 to 10

2 envelopes unflavored gelatin
2½ cups orange juice
1 tablespoon grated orange peel
1 cup heavy cream, whipped
3 egg whites

In a saucepan, sprinkle gelatin over orange juice. Heat over low heat until gelatin completely dissolves. Remove from heat and stir in orange peel. Chill just until mixture resembles custard but is not set, about 40 minutes. Beat with a wire whisk until foamy. Fold in whipped cream. Beat egg whites until stiff and glossy and fold in. Turn into a 6-cup gelatin mold and refrigerate for 3½ hours until set. Unmold to serve.

Preparation Time: 10 minutes
Chilling Time: 4½ hours

Approximately 225 calories per serving
Approximately 20 grams carbohydrate per serving

SWEET POTATO AND BANANA CASSEROLE
Serves 12

1 quart water
6 peeled sweet potatoes or yams
6 ripe bananas
1 tablespoon lemon juice or
   pineapple juice
½ cup orange juice
2 teaspoons grated orange peel
1 cup apple juice
1 teaspoon cinnamon
1 tablespoon cornstarch

Bring water to a gentle boil. Add sweet potatoes or yams and cook for 30 minutes until vegetable can be easily pierced with a fork. Drain and slice. Set aside.

Preheat oven to 375 degrees. Slice bananas and toss with lemon juice to prevent discoloring. In a 2-quart soufflé dish or casserole, arrange sweet potato or yam slices and bananas in alternating layers, ending with a layer of bananas. With remaining sweet potato or yam slices, decorate the top of the casserole, overlapping slices slightly.

In a bowl, combine orange juice, orange peel, apple juice, cinnamon and cornstarch. Pour over casserole, cover and bake for 45 minutes until sauce is thick.

Preparation Time: 40 minutes
Baking Time: 45 minutes

Approximately 150 calories per serving
Over 35 grams carbohydrate per serving

HALLOWEEN COMPOTE
Serves 12 to 15

1 pound fresh chestnuts
5 cups water
1 5-pound pumpkin, seeded,
   peeled and cut into 1-inch
   pieces
2 cups apple juice

With a sharp knife, cut slits in chestnuts. Boil in water for 15 minutes and remove shells. Peel pieces of pumpkin with a vegetable peeler, chop into 1 inch cubes, and add to cooking chestnuts. Cook 30 minutes. Stir in remaining ingredients and cook for 1 hour until sauce is thick. Serve from a soup caldron.

8 apples, sliced
⅔ cup raisins
1 teaspoon cinnamon
½ teaspoon ground ginger
1 teaspoon ground cardamom

Preparation Time: 20 minutes
Cooking Time: 90 minutes

Approximately 150 calories per serving
Over 35 grams carbohydrate per serving

PUMPKIN SOUFFLÉ

Serves 10 to 12

1½ pound pumpkin, seeded, peeled and cut into 1-inch cubes
1 quart boiling water
5 eggs, separated
⅔ cup frozen orange juice concentrate, thawed
3 tablespoons pineapple juice
½ teaspoon ground ginger
½ teaspoon ground cloves
½ teaspoon ground nutmeg
1 teaspoon cinnamon

Preheat oven to 350 degrees. Place pumpkin in boiling water and cook for 30 minutes until soft. Drain pumpkin and mash pulp. Cool. Beat in egg yolks, orange juice concentrate, pineapple juice, ginger, cloves, nutmeg and cinnamon. Beat egg whites until stiff and glossy. Fold into pumpkin mixture. Turn into a buttered 6-cup soufflé dish and bake for 40 to 45 minutes until lightly browned.

Preparation Time: 45 minutes
Baking Time: 40 to 45 minutes

Approximately 150 calories per serving
Approximately 20 grams carbohydrate per serving

PUMPKIN PARFAIT

Serves 8

1 envelope unflavored gelatin
¼ cup frozen apple juice concentrate, thawed
4 eggs, separated
1¼ cups pumpkin purée*
1 cup milk
½ teaspoon cinnamon
¼ teaspoon ground nutmeg
¼ teaspoon ground ginger
1½ tablespoons cornstarch or arrowroot starch

Preparation Time: 60 minutes
Chilling Time: 3½ hours

Sprinkle gelatin over apple juice concentrate to dissolve. Set aside. In a saucepan, combine egg yolks, pumpkin purée, milk, cinnamon, nutmeg, ginger and cornstarch. Cook, stirring occasionally, until mixture thickens. Remove from heat and immediately stir in gelatin and concentrate mixture. Refrigerate for 45 minutes until mixture is consistency of custard but not set.

Beat egg whites until stiff and glossy. Beat pumpkin mixture with a wire whisk. Fold stiff whites into pumpkin mixture. Pour into a gelatin mold or individual parfait glasses and chill for 3 to 3½ hours until set. If using mold, unmold to serve.

Approximately 150 calories per serving
Approximately 20 grams carbohydrate per serving

* Pumpkin purée with no sugar added can be found canned in grocery stores. It can also be made at home by seeding a pumpkin, cutting it into 4-inch pieces and steaming the pieces until soft. Once steamed, the skin will come off easily, and the pieces can be puréed in an electric blender or food processor.

GLAZED ORANGES

Serves 12

⅓ cup liquid barley malt
⅔ cup water
1 tablespoon frozen orange juice concentrate, thawed
1 teaspoon grated orange peel

In a saucepan, gently boil malt, water, orange juice concentrate, orange peel and cinnamon for 15 minutes. Pour mixture over orange wedges and toss. Place in a decorative bowl and sprinkle with slivered almonds.

1 teaspoon cinnamon
6 oranges, peeled and in sec-
    tions
2 tablespoons slivered almonds

Cooking Time: 15 minutes
Preparation Time: 10 minutes

Approximately 150 calories per serving
Over 35 grams carbohydrate per serving

CARROT PUDDING
Serves 8

3 cups grated carrots
⅓ cup raisins or currants
⅔ cup frozen pineapple juice
    concentrate, thawed
4 eggs, lightly beaten
2 cups milk, scalded and cooled
    to lukewarm
1 tablespoon soy flour
1 teaspoon cinnamon

Preheat oven to 350 degrees. Cover the bottom of a buttered 6-cup soufflé dish with grated carrots and raisins. Beat together pineapple juice concentrate, eggs, milk, soy flour and cinnamon in a bowl. Pour over carrots. Place soufflé dish in 1 inch of hot water and bake for 45 to 50 minutes until a knife inserted into the center of the pudding comes out clean.

Preparation Time: 15 minutes
Baking Time: 45 to 50 minutes

Approximately 150 calories per serving
Over 30 grams carbohydrate per serving

ORANGE MERINGUE PIE
Serves 8

½ Flaky Pie Dough recipe (see
    p. 16)
4 tablespoons arrowroot or
    cornstarch
4 tablespoons brown rice flour
1½ cups orange juice

Preheat oven to to 350 degrees. Prepare dough. Roll and line a 9-inch pie plate. Bake for 20 minutes.

In a saucepan, combine starch, flour, orange juice and egg yolks. Cook without boiling, stirring occasionally, until mixture thickens to the consistency of thick custard. Remove from heat.

4 eggs, separated
1 tablespoon grated orange peel
½ teaspoon orange extract

Beat egg whites and orange peel until foamy. Add orange extract and beat until stiff and glossy. Pour custard into baked pie shell. Top with meringue and bake for 10 minutes until meringue is lightly browned at tips. Cool before serving.

Preparation Time: 30 minutes
Baking Time: 10 minutes

Under 150 calories per serving
Approximately 20 grams carbohydrate per serving

ORANGE-CRANBERRY TORTE
Serves 12

CAKE INGREDIENTS
¼ cup oil
3 eggs, separated
1 cup orange juice
¼ cup liquid barley malt
1 tablespoon grated orange peel
3 tablespoons frozen apple
  juice concentrate, thawed
1 cup whole wheat pastry flour
1 cup brown rice flour
⅓ cup non-instant skim milk
  powder
1½ teaspoons baking soda

CRANBERRY FILLING INGREDIENTS
1 cup fresh whole cranberries
1½ cups apple juice

Preheat oven to 350 degrees. In a bowl, beat oil, egg yolks, orange juice, barley malt, orange peel and apple juice concentrate. In a separate bowl, mix pastry flour, brown rice flour, milk powder and baking soda with a wire whisk. Gradually stir dry mixture into liquid ingredients to form a smooth batter. Beat egg whites until stiff and fold into batter. Pour into an oiled 9-inch springform pan. Bake for 1½ hours until a toothpick inserted into the center of the cake comes out clean. Run a knife around the edge of cake and remove springform. Allow cake to cool while preparing fillings.

To prepare cranberry filling, combine cranberries and apple juice in a saucepan. Cook until cranberries pop. Mash cranberries in juice. Stir in apple juice concentrate and bring to a gentle boil. Stir in starch-and-water paste. Continue stirring for 3 minutes until mixture thickens. Remove from heat and stir in orange peel.

2 tablespoons frozen apple juice concentrate, thawed

2 tablespoons cornstarch or arrowroot starch mixed with 2 tablespoons water

1 tablespoon grated orange peel

ORANGE CREAM FILLING

1½ cups part-skim milk ricotta cheese

2 tablespoons frozen orange juice concentrate, thawed

1 tablespoon grated orange peel

GARNISH INGREDIENTS

1 orange, unpeeled, cut in half lengthwise and sliced

16 whole cranberries

Preparation Time: 30 minutes
Baking Time: 90 minutes
Assembling Time: 15 minutes

To prepare orange cream filling, blend ricotta, orange juice concentrate and orange peel in an electric blender or food processor until smooth.

Slice cake in half to form 2 layers. Spread first layer with half cranberry topping and half cream filling. Cover with second layer of cake. Top with remaining cranberry mixture and remaining cream mixture. Place orange wedges and cranberries around the edge of cake.

Approximately 225 calories per serving
Over 35 grams carbohydrate per serving

PUMPKIN CAKE

Serves 10 to 12

CAKE INGREDIENTS

⅓ cup oil

2 cups pumpkin purée (see p. 146)

¼ cup frozen apple juice concentrate, thawed

¼ cup liquid barley malt

5 eggs, separated

Preheat oven to to 350 degrees. In a bowl, beat oil, pumpkin purée, apple juice concentrate, malt, egg yolks and raisins or currants. In a separate bowl, mix brown rice flour, whole wheat flour, milk powder, baking powder and pumpkin pie spice with a wire whisk until thoroughly combined. Stir dry mixture into liquids to form a smooth batter. Beat egg whites until stiff and fold into batter. Pour into 2 well-oiled and

⅓ cup raisins or currants
1¼ cups brown rice flour
1¼ cups whole wheat pastry
　flour
⅓ cup non-instant skim milk
　powder
2 teaspoons baking powder
2 teaspoons pumpkin pie spice

FROSTING INGREDIENTS
¼ cup soft unsalted butter
1½ cups non-instant skim milk
　powder
½ cup orange juice
½ teaspoon cinnamon
¼ teaspoon ground ginger

Preparation Time: 20 minutes
Baking Time: 1 hour
Frosting Time: 5 minutes

dusted 9-inch cake pans. Bake for 1 hour. Cool for 10 minutes. Remove from pans and place on wire racks to cool thoroughly before frosting.

To prepare frosting, blend butter, milk powder, orange juice, cinnamon and ginger in an electric blender or food processor until smooth and thick. If frosting is too thin add milk powder 1 teaspoon at a time until desired thickness is reached. Frost cake.

Approximately 225 calories per serving
Over 35 grams carbohydrate per serving

SWEET POTATO CAKE WITH RAISIN SAUCE　　*Serves 12 to 15*

CAKE INGREDIENTS
⅓ cup oil
5 eggs, separated
2 cups orange juice
¼ cup liquid barley malt
1⅓ cups whole wheat pastry
　flour
1⅓ cups brown rice flour
3 tablespoons gluten flour

Preheat oven to 350 degrees. In a bowl, beat oil, egg yolks, orange juice and liquid barley malt. In a separate bowl, mix pastry flour, brown rice flour, gluten flour, baking soda and cinnamon. Gradually stir dry mixture into liquids to form a smooth batter. Stir in sweet potato and orange peel. Pour into a well-oiled and dusted tube or bundt pan. Bake for 1 hour until a toothpick inserted into cake comes out clean. Cool slightly and remove from pan.

1½ teaspoons baking soda
1 teaspoon cinnamon
1 cup grated sweet potato
1 tablespoon grated orange peel

SAUCE INGREDIENTS
1 cup raisins
2 cups apple juice
1 cup orange juice
3 tablespoons cornstarch
2 teaspoons grated orange rind

Preparation Time: 20 minutes
Baking Time: 90 minutes

To prepare sauce, combine raisins, apple juice, orange juice, cornstarch and orange peel in a saucepan. Heat, stirring occasionally, until sauce thickens. Serve warm with cake.

Approximately 225 calories per serving
Over 35 grams carbohydrate per serving

OPEN FACE ORANGE CAKE

Serves 12

CAKE INGREDIENTS
¼ cup oil
3 eggs, separated
1 cup orange juice
¼ cup liquid barley malt
⅔ cup brown rice flour
⅔ cup whole wheat pastry flour
1½ teaspoons baking powder
2 teaspoons grated orange peel

TOPPING INGREDIENTS
¾ cup apple juice
1 teaspoon cinnamon
1 tablespoon tapioca

Preheat oven to 350 degrees. In a bowl, beat oil, egg yolks, orange juice and liquid barley malt. In a separate bowl, mix rice flour, whole wheat pastry flour and baking powder with a wire whisk until well combined. Stir dry ingredients gradually into liquids to form a smooth batter. Stir in orange peel. Beat egg whites until stiff and fold into batter. Pour batter into an oiled 10-inch springform pan and bake for 1 hour until a toothpick inserted into the center comes out clean. Run a knife around the outer edge of the cake and remove springform.

To make topping, heat apple juice, cinnamon and tapioca over low heat, stirring occasionally, until mixture thickens. Stir in oranges and cook for 5 minutes until heated through. Remove from heat and cool

3 oranges, peeled, halved and
  thinly sliced
Small cluster purple grapes

Preparation Time: 30 minutes
Baking Time: 1 hour

slightly. Arrange glazed orange halves in overlapping concentric circles on cake. Place purple grapes in the center of the cake.

Approximately 225 calories per serving
Over 35 grams carbohydrate per serving

ORANGE CHEESECAKE

Serves 12 to 16

Crumble Crust recipe (see p. 17)

3 eggs, separated
⅔ cup frozen apple juice concentrate, thawed
1 teaspoon almond extract
2 cups part-skim milk ricotta cheese
3 tablespoons frozen orange juice concentrate, thawed
2 tablespoons soy flour
1 cup small curd cottage cheese
2 teaspoons grated orange peel

1 cup part-skim milk ricotta cheese blended with 2 tablespoons orange juice concentrate (in an electric blender)
1 orange, unpeeled, halved lengthwise and thinly sliced

Preheat oven to 350 degrees. Line 10-inch springform pan with crumble crust mixture and bake for 10 minutes until lightly browned. Remove from oven.

In an electric blender, beat egg yolks, apple juice concentrate, almond extract, ricotta, orange juice concentrate, soy flour, cottage cheese and grated orange peel until smooth and light. Pour into a bowl. Beat egg whites until stiff and glossy. Fold into cheesecake batter. Pour into crust and bake for 50 to 60 minutes until a knife inserted into the center comes out clean. Cool for 10 minutes. Run a knife around the edge of cake. Remove springform. Spread ricotta and orange juice concentrate mixture over cake. Place unpeeled orange slices around edge of cake. Cool completely before serving.

Preparation Time: 15 minutes
Baking Time: 50 to 60 minutes

Approximately 225 calories per serving
Approximately 20 grams carbohydrate per serving

APPLE BUTTER CUSTARD
Serves 8

4 eggs, lightly beaten
1 teaspoon cinnamon
¼ cup apple butter
2 teaspoons grated orange peel
2 teaspoons soy flour
3 cups milk, scalded and cooled
    to lukewarm

Preheat oven to 350 degrees. Beat together all ingredients. Pour into a lightly oiled 4-cup soufflé dish. Place in a pan filled with an inch of hot water and bake for 45 minutes until set.

Preparation Time: 10 minutes
Baking Time: 45 minutes

Approximately 150 calories per serving
Approximately 20 grams carbohydrate per serving

YAM PUDDING
Serves 10

3 yams, grated
¼ cup frozen apple juice concentrate, thawed
2 tablespoons blackstrap molasses
3 eggs
1½ cups milk
¼ cup non-instant milk powder
1 tablespoon soy flour
2 teaspoons vanilla
1 tablespoon butter, melted

Preheat oven to 350 degrees. Beat together all ingredients. Pour into a lightly oiled 4-cup soufflé dish. Place in an inch of hot water and bake for 1 hour until set.

Preparation Time: 15 minutes
Baking Time: 1 hour

Approximately 150 calories per serving
Approximately 20 grams carbohydrate per serving

HALLOWEEN ORANGE BALLS
Makes 58

1 cup sugarless cake or cookie crumbs
¾ cup unsweetened shredded coconut
1 teaspoon grated orange peel
½ cup orange juice
¾ cup non-instant skim milk powder
3 tablespoons soft unsalted butter
½ teaspoon orange extract
½ cup ground almonds

Preparation Time: 15 minutes
Chilling Time: Overnight

Combine crumbs, coconut, grated orange peel, orange juice, milk powder, soft butter and orange extract to form a soft dough. Form into teaspoon-size balls and roll in ground nuts. Cover and allow to stand in refrigerator overnight until firm.

As a Halloween gift place in a plastic jack-o'-lantern. These confections should be kept refrigerated.

Under 150 calories per candy
Under 20 grams carbohydrate per candy

POPCORN FUDGE
Makes 24 squares

⅓ cup soft butter
1½ cups non-instant skim milk powder
⅓ cup frozen apple juice concentrate, thawed
1 teaspoon almond extract
3 cups popped popcorn

Preparation Time: 15 minutes
Setting Time: Overnight

In a blender or food processor, blend butter, milk powder, apple juice concentrate and almond extract until smooth. Pour over popcorn and stir to coat thoroughly. Turn onto an oiled 9 x 12-inch pan, cover and refrigerate overnight. Cut into 24 rectangles.

This unusual fudge makes a delicious Halloween gift if placed in a plastic jack-o'-lantern. It should be kept refrigerated.

Approximately 150 calories per serving
Under 30 grams carbohydrate per serving

CARROT COOKIES

Makes 36

COOKIE INGREDIENTS
¾ cup oil
2 eggs
1 cup cooked mashed carrots
3 tablespoons frozen apple
  juice concentrate, thawed
1¼ cups raw wheat germ
1 cup whole wheat pastry flour
2 teaspoons baking powder

FROSTING INGREDIENTS
¼ cup soft unsalted butter
1½ cups non-instant milk powder
½ cup pineapple juice

Preparation Time: 15 minutes
Baking Time: 15 minutes

Preheat oven to 375 degrees. To make cookies, beat oil, eggs, mashed carrots and apple juice concentrate together. In a separate bowl, mix wheat germ, pastry flour and baking powder. Mix dry combination into liquids to form a cookie batter. Drop by spoonfuls onto an oiled baking sheet. Bake for 15 minutes just until edges are lightly browned.

While cookies cool, make frosting. Blend butter, milk powder and pineapple juice in an electric blender or food processor until smooth. Frost cookies.

As a gift, these cookies can be placed in a glass or tin container, wrapped in orange cellophane and tied with a black bow.

Under 150 calories per serving
Under 30 grams carbohydrate per serving

PUMPKIN COOKIES

Makes 48

½ cup oil
½ cup apple or orange juice
2½ teaspoons vanilla
1 cup raisins
2 cups pumpkin purée (see p. 146)
2 teaspoons baking powder

Preheat oven to 375 degrees. Beat oil, juice, vanilla, raisins and pumpkin purée. In a separate bowl, mix baking powder, cinnamon, wheat germ, and pastry flour. Gradually stir dry mixture into liquids to form a cookie batter. Drop by tablespoons onto a well-oiled baking sheet and bake for 12 minutes until edges are lightly browned. Cool and remove from baking sheet.

4 teaspoons cinnamon
2 cups raw wheat germ
2 cups whole wheat pastry flour

Preparation Time: 15 minutes
Baking Time: 12 minutes

Place in a plastic jack-o'-lantern for a Halloween gift or centerpiece

Under 150 calories per serving
Under 30 grams carbohydrate per serving

ORANGE HAYSTACKS
Makes 24

1 egg
1 tablespoon melted butter
3 tablespoons frozen orange
  juice concentrate, thawed
2 tablespoons whole wheat
  pastry flour
2 cups unsweetened shredded
  coconut

Preparation Time: 10 minutes
Baking Time: 20 minutes

Preheat oven to 350 degrees. Beat egg, butter and orange juice concentrate. Stir in flour and coconut. Fill an oiled eggcup with dough to form a "haystack," then turn onto a well-oiled baking sheet. Repeat until all dough is used. Bake for 20 minutes until lightly browned.

To use as a gift, place in a tin and wrap in Halloween paper.

Under 150 calories per serving
Under 20 grams carbohydrate per serving

ORANGE CREAM PUFFS
Serves 12

Cream Puff Pastry recipe (see
  p. 19)

FILLING INGREDIENTS
2 eggs
⅔ cup frozen orange juice concentrate, thawed
4 tablespoons cornstarch

Preheat oven to 425 degrees. Drop cream puff dough by tablespoonfuls onto a baking sheet sprayed with non-stick vegetable spray. Bake for 40 minutes until puffed and golden. Turn off oven and leave puffs in until both oven and pastry have cooled.

To make filling, combine eggs, orange juice concentrate and cornstarch in a saucepan. Heat without boiling, stirring constantly, until mixture thickens. Gradually stir in lukewarm milk. Continue to cook

2 cups milk, scalded and cooled
  to lukewarm
1 teaspoon grated orange peel
1 teaspoon vanilla

FROSTING INGREDIENTS
¼ cup soft unsalted butter
1½ cups non-instant milk powder
⅔ cup orange juice
1 teaspoon grated orange peel

Preparation Time: 20 minutes
Baking Time: 90 minutes

until mixture reaches the consistency of thick custard. Remove from heat and stir in orange peel and vanilla. Cool before filling puffs. Cut puffs in half and remove any soft dough inside. Spoon custard into bottom half and cover with top half of pastry.

Make frosting by blending butter, milk powder, orange juice and orange peel in an electric blender or food processor until smooth. Frost puffs.

These make a lovely gift if placed in a decorative Halloween box and tied with an orange or black bow. Be sure to keep puffs refrigerated.

Approximately 225 calories per serving
Approximately 30 grams carbohydrate per serving

PUMPKIN TARTS

Makes 16 tarts

Flaky Pastry Dough or Stretchy
  Pastry Dough recipe (see p.
  16)
2 cups pumpkin purée (see p.
  146)
¼ cup frozen apple juice concentrate, thawed
2 teaspoons cinnamon
½ teaspoon ground ginger
¼ teaspoon ground cloves
1¼ cups milk
¼ cup non-instant skim milk
  powder

Preparation Time: 20 minutes
Baking Time: 20 minutes

Divide dough into 16 parts. Place each part on a 3½-inch square of heavy duty aluminum foil. Roll each piece of dough into a circle, 3½ inches in diameter. With pastry scissors, trim foil and dough to form a neat circle. Shape foil and pastry together to form tarts with 1-inch edges. Flute edges.

To make filling for tart shells, beat pumpkin purée, apple juice concentrate, cinnamon, ginger, cloves, milk and milk powder until smooth. Pour into tarts and bake at 425 degrees for 10 minutes and at 350 degrees for an additional 10 minutes, until filling has set.

For a Halloween gift, place tarts in a decorative orange box and tie with a black ribbon.

Approximately 150 calories per serving
Under 30 grams carbohydrate per serving

Children's Trick-O'-Treats

PEANUT BUTTER POPCORN BALLS
Makes 32 balls

1 cup liquid barley malt
4 tablespoons oil or melted butter
6 tablespoons peanut butter
8 cups popped popcorn

Preparation and Cooking Time: 15 minutes

In a large pan, mix malt, oil and peanut butter until well combined. Heat for 10 minutes until mixture bubbles. Pour in popped corn and stir until well coated. Moisten hands with water and shape into balls pressing firmly.

Approximately 225 calories per serving
Over 35 grams carbohydrate per serving

CARAMEL APPLES
Serves 10 to 12

1 cup liquid barley malt
1 cup milk
3 tablespoons non-instant skim milk powder
10 to 12 apples with sticks inserted

Preparation and Cooking Time: 30 minutes

In a saucepan, combine malt, milk and milk powder. Cook, stirring occasionally, until mixture boils gently. Continue to boil for 20 minutes or until mixture reaches soft-ball stage. Dip apples in mixture and place on wax paper to cool.

Approximately 225 calories per serving
Over 35 grams carbohydrate per serving

PEANUT BUTTER CARAMEL APPLES

Serves 10 to 12

1 cup liquid barley malt
1 cup milk
2 tablespoons non-instant skim
  milk powder
3 tablespoons peanut butter
½ cup finely chopped peanuts
10 to 12 apples with sticks inserted

In a saucepan, combine malt, milk, and milk powder. Heat to a gentle boil. Continue to boil for 20 minutes until mixture reaches soft-ball stage. Stir in peanut butter. Dip apples in mixture, then roll them in chopped peanuts. Place on wax paper to harden.

Preparation and Cooking Time:
35 minutes

Approximately 225 calories per serving
Over 35 grams carbohydrate per serving

CORN AND PEANUT "JACKS"

Serves 8 to 10

½ cup liquid barley malt
¼ cup oil or melted butter
3 cups popped popcorn
1 cup shelled roasted peanuts

In a large pan, heat malt and oil or melted butter to boiling. Boil for 5 minutes, stirring constantly. Add popcorn and peanuts. Stir to coat thoroughly. Turn onto wax paper and cool. Break up with hands and place individual portions in small trick-o'-treat bags.

Preparation and Cooking Time:
15 minutes

Approximately 225 calories per serving
Over 35 grams carbohydrate per serving

CAROB COCONUT CANDIED APPLES

Serves 10 to 12

1 cup liquid barley malt
1 cup milk
3 tablespoons carob powder
10 to 12 apples with sticks inserted
½ cup unsweetened shredded coconut

In a saucepan, combine malt, milk and carob powder. Bring to a gentle boil and continue to boil for 20 minutes until soft-ball stage is reached. Dip apples, roll in coconut and place on wax paper to harden.

Preparation and Cooking Time: 35 minutes

Approximately 225 calories per serving
Over 35 grams carbohydrate per serving

9

A Thanksgiving Harvest of Naturally Sweet Desserts

CARAMEL PUMPKIN FLAN

Serves 10

1 cup pumpkin purée (see p. 146)

1½ cups milk

½ cup frozen apple juice concentrate, thawed

1 tablespoon non-instant skim milk powder

1 teaspoon soy flour

6 eggs, slightly beaten

2 tablespoons vanilla

¼ cup liquid barley malt

2 tablespoons water

Preparation Time: 15 minutes
Baking Time: 50 to 60 minutes
Chilling Time: Overnight

In a saucepan, heat pumpkin purée, milk, apple juice concentrate and milk powder to a gentle boil. Beat together soy flour and eggs. Stir ½ cup of pumpkin mixture into eggs. Gradually stir this mixture into heated pumpkin mixture. Stir in vanilla. Pour into a lightly oiled quiche pan. Place in a pan filled with ¾-inch hot water and bake for 50 to 60 minutes until set. Refrigerate overnight. In a saucepan, bring malt and water to a boil for 10 minutes until soft-ball stage is reached. Drizzle malt mixture over flan in a crisscross design. Cool before serving.

Approximately 150 calories per serving
Approximately 30 grams carbohydrate per serving

BAKED CRANBERRY APPLE DUMPLINGS
with Cranberry Applesauce

Serves 10 to 12

Flaky Pastry Dough or Stretchy Pastry Dough recipe (see p. 16)

Roll out dough and cut into 4-inch squares. Combine grated apples, cinnamon, orange peel, raisins, cranberries, apple juice concentrate and cornstarch. Spoon equal portions of filling on each square. Bring the corners of squares together and pinch.

FILLING INGREDIENTS
5 apples, unpeeled, and grated
¼ teaspoon cinnamon
2 teaspoons grated orange peel
¼ cup raisins
⅓ cup whole fresh cranberries
2 tablespoons frozen apple
  juice concentrate, thawed
3 tablespoons cornstarch or arrowroot starch
2 egg yolks, beaten

SAUCE INGREDIENTS
1 cup whole fresh cranberries
¼ cup frozen apple juice concentrate, thawed
2 cups apple juice
3 tablespoons cornstarch or arrowroot starch dissolved in 3
  tablespoons water

Preparation Time: 30 minutes
Baking Time: 20 to 25 minutes

Preheat oven to 350 degrees. Brush dumplings with egg yolk and bake for 20 to 25 minutes until golden brown.

To make sauce, combine cranberries, apple juice concentrate and apple juice in a saucepan. Heat to boiling. Mash cranberries when they begin to pop. Stir in cornstarch-and-water paste. Continue stirring for 3 minutes until sauce thickens. Serve sauce warm over dumplings.

Approximately 150 calories per serving
Under 30 grams carbohydrate per serving

ORANGE CRANBERRY MOLD

Serves 10 to 12

2 envelopes unflavored gelatin
½ cup orange juice
1½ cups whole fresh cranberries
2 cups apple juice
¼ cup frozen apple juice concentrate, thawed

In a cup, stir gelatin into orange juice and set aside. In a saucepan, combine cranberries, apple juice and apple juice concentrate. Bring to a gentle boil. Mash cranberries when they begin to pop. Stir in oranges and orange peel and remove from heat. Stir in gelatin and orange juice mixture. Pour into a 6-cup gelatin mold and refrigerate for 6 to 8 hours until set. Unmold to serve.

3 oranges, peeled with membranes removed
2 teaspoons grated orange peel

Preparation Time: 10 minutes
Chilling Time: 6 to 8 hours

Under 150 calories per serving
Approximately 30 grams carbohydrate per serving

APPLE FRITTERS WITH SESAME SAUCE

Serves 18

FRITTER INGREDIENTS

2 cups boiling apple juice
1 cup corn flour
1 cup cooked brown rice
3 apples, unpeeled and grated
¼ cup arrowroot or cornstarch
2 tablespoons chestnut flour
1 teaspoon cinnamon
½ teaspoon ground ginger
½ teaspoon ground allspice
Oil for frying

SAUCE INGREDIENTS

¼ cup sesame tahini
¼ cup brown rice flour
2 cups apple juice
1 teaspoon vanilla
1 teaspoon grated lemon peel

Preparation Time: 15 minutes
Frying Time: 20 minutes

Stir boiling apple juice into corn flour. Add brown rice, grated apples, cornstarch, chestnut flour, cinnamon, ginger and allspice. Heat 2 inches of oil to frying temperature. Drop batter by spoonfuls into hot oil and deep-fry on both sides until lightly browned. Drain on paper towels.

To make sauce, combine sesame tahini, rice flour, apple juice, vanilla and lemon peel in a saucepan. Heat over medium heat, stirring occasionally, until mixture thickens and there is no taste of raw flour. Serve sauce alongside fritters.

Approximately 150 calories per serving
Approximately 30 grams carbohydrate per serving

FRENCH FRIED APPLE RINGS

Serves 8

4 large unpeeled apples, cored
  and sliced ¼-inch thick
3 tablespoons soy flour
⅔ cup apple juice
½ cup whole wheat pastry flour
1½ tablespoons arrowroot or
  cornstarch
1 teaspoon ground cardamom
½ teaspoon cinnamon
Oil for frying

Preparation Time: 10 minutes
Frying Time: 15 minutes

Place apples and soy flour in a paper bag and shake to coat apples. In an electric blender or food processor, blend apple juice, pastry flour, cornstarch, cardamom and cinnamon. Heat 2 inches of oil to deep-frying temperature, until water sizzles when sprinkled on it. Dip apples in batter and deep-fry on both sides until golden brown. Drain on paper towels.

Approximately 150 calories per serving
Under 30 grams carbohydrate per serving

YAM APPLESAUCE PIE

Serves 8

Crumble Crust recipe (see p. 17)
2 cups peeled, chopped yams
1 inch fresh ginger, sliced
2 cups apple juice
3 tablespoons cornstarch or arrowroot starch
3 eggs, beaten
1½ cups unsweetened applesauce

Preparation Time: 40 minutes
Baking Time: 40 minutes

Preheat oven to 375 degrees. Prepare crust. Line a 9-inch springform pan. Bake for 10–15 minutes until lightly browned.

Prepare filling. In a saucepan, cook yams, ginger and apple juice until yams are soft. Blend until smooth in an electric blender or food processor. Stir in cornstarch, eggs and applesauce. Pour into shell. Bake for 40 minutes until firm. Cool to serve.

Approximately 150 calories per serving
Approximately 30 grams carbohydrate per serving

INDIAN PUDDING

Serves 8

⅔ cup cornmeal
3 cups apple juice
½ cup raisins or currants
2 tablespoons blackstrap molasses
2 apples, peeled and grated
4 tablespoons soy flour
1 teaspoon cinnamon
2 eggs, beaten

Preparation Time: 30 minutes
Baking Time: 1 hour

In a frying pan, dry-roast cornmeal over medium heat until it is lightly browned. Add apple juice and raisins and cook for 15 minutes. Cool.

Preheat oven to 350 degrees. Add molasses, grated apple, soy flour, cinnamon and eggs to cornmeal and stir. Pour into an oiled 4-cup casserole and bake for 1 hour. Serve warm alone or with milk.

Approximately 150 calories per serving
Under 30 grams carbohydrate per serving

TAHINI, WALNUT, COFFEE PARFAITS

Serves 6 to 8

TAHINI CUSTARD INGREDIENTS

3 cups apple juice
¼ cup sesame tahini
4 tablespoons cornstarch
1 teaspoon vanilla

COFFEE WALNUT SAUCE INGREDIENTS

1½ cups water
3 tablespoons apple butter

In a saucepan, combine apple juice, tahini, and cornstarch. Beat until well combined. Heat over medium heat, stirring occasionally, until mixture thickens to the texture of custard. Remove from heat, stir in vanilla and cool to lukewarm.

In another saucepan, mix water, apple butter, grain coffee substitute, raisins or currants and cornstarch. Heat over medium heat, stirring occasionally, until mixture thickens. Remove from heat and stir in walnuts. In parfait glasses, alternate layer of custard and sauce.

1 tablespoon instant grain coffee substitute
¼ cup raisins or currants
2 tablespoons cornstarch
¾ cup walnut pieces

Preparation Time: 20 minutes
Assembling Time: 10 minutes

Approximately 150 calories per serving
Approximately 30 grams carbohydrate per serving

BAKED PEARS IN ORANGE SAUCE

Serves 12

6 pears, halved and cored
1 cup orange juice
½ teaspoon cinnamon
2 teaspoons grated orange peel
1 tablespoon sesame tahini
2 teaspoons cornstarch or arrowroot starch dissolved in 2
teaspoons water

Preheat oven to 350 degrees. Place pears in a shallow baking dish. Mix orange juice, cinnamon and orange peel. Pour over pears. Cover and bake for 30 minutes until pears are easily pierced with a fork. Pour off liquids into a saucepan. Beat in tahini and bring to a gentle boil. Stir in starch-and-water paste. Continue stirring for 3 minutes until mixture thickens. Pour over pears and serve while warm.

Preparation Time: 10 minutes
Baking Time: 30 minutes

Under 150 calories per serving
Approximately 20 grams carbohydrate per serving

CLASSIC PUMPKIN PIE

Serves 8

½ Flaky Pastry Dough recipe
(see p. 16)
3 eggs, lightly beaten
1¼ cups pumpkin purée (see p.
146)
⅓ cup frozen apple juice concentrate, thawed
1 teaspoon cinnamon
1 teaspoon ground cardamom

Preheat oven to 425 degrees. Roll pie dough and line a 9-inch pie plate.

In an electric blender or food processor, blend eggs, pumpkin purée, apple juice concentrate, cinnamon, cardamom, ginger, cloves, orange peel, milk powder and milk until smooth. Pour into lined pie plate and bake at 425 for 15 minutes. Reduce heat to 350 degrees and bake for 45 minutes until firm. Cool to serve.

½ teaspoon ground ginger
½ teaspoon ground cloves
1 teaspoon grated orange peel
¼ cup non-instant skim milk
   powder
1 cup milk or skim milk

Preparation Time: 20 minutes
Baking Time: 1 hour

Under 125 calories per serving
Approximately 20 grams carbohydrate per serving

"MINCEMEAT" PIE

Serves 8

1½ cups raisins
1 cup apple juice

3 tablespoons cornstarch or arrowroot starch dissolved in 3
   tablespoons water
3 cups finely diced unpeeled
   apples
¾ cup chopped walnuts
1 tablespoon grated orange peel
1 tablespoons frozen orange
   juice concentrate, thawed
1 teaspoon cinnamon
½ teaspoon ground ginger
Flaky Pastry Dough recipe
   (see p. 16)

Preparation Time: Overnight plus
20 minutes
Baking Time: 40 minutes

Soak raisins in apple juice overnight.

    Preheat oven to 375 degrees. In an electric blender or food processor, blend raisins and apple juice until smooth. In a saucepan, bring mixture to a gentle boil. Remove from heat and stir in starch-and-water paste, apples, walnuts, orange peel, orange juice concentrate, cinnamon and ginger.

    Roll dough for crusts into 2 12-inch circles. Line a 9-inch pie plate with one. Pour in filling. With a sharp knife, cut the other pastry into ¾-inch strips. Put one short strip over the side of the pie. Put another short strip perpendicular to the first. Repeat, alternately, strips perpendicular to one another to create a lattice-top crust. Bake for 40 minutes until lightly browned.

Approximately 150 calories per serving
Over 35 grams carbohydrate per serving

CHESTNUT APPLE PIE

Serves 8

2 cups whole fresh chestnuts
3 cups water
1 cup apple juice
3 tablespoons cornstarch dissolved in 3 tablespoons water
2 cups sliced, unpeeled apples
2 teaspoons grated orange peel
Flaky Pastry Dough recipe (see p. 16)

With a sharp knife, slit chestnuts. Boil in water for 15 minutes. Peel chestnuts. Place chestnuts and apple juice in a saucepan and gently boil for 20 minutes. Stir in cornstarch-and-water paste, apples and orange peel. Continue stirring for 3 minutes until mixture thickens. Remove from heat and set aside.

Roll pastry dough into 2 12-inch circles. Line a 9-inch pie plate with one pastry. Pour filling into lined plate. Cover with second pastry. Flute edges and cut slits in top crust for steam to escape. Bake for 40 minutes at 400 degrees until lightly browned.

Preparation Time: 25 minutes
Baking Time: 40 minutes

Approximately 150 calories per serving
Over 35 grams carbohydrate per serving

APPLE CRANBERRY NUT PIE

Serves 8

2 cups whole fresh cranberries
2 cups grated, sweet, unpeeled apples
½ cup chopped walnuts
4 tablespoons quick-cooking tapioca
½ cup frozen apple juice concentrate, thawed
Flaky Pastry Dough or Stretchy Pastry Dough recipe (see p. 16)

Preheat oven to 450 degrees. In a bowl, combine cranberries, apples, walnuts, tapioca and apple juice concentrate.

Roll dough into 2 12-inch circles. Line a 9-inch pie plate with one. Pour in filling. Cover with second pastry. Flute edges and cut slits in top for steam to escape. Bake at 450 for 10 minutes; reduce heat to 350 and continue baking for 35 minutes until golden brown. Cool at least 2 hours before serving.

Preparation Time: 25 minutes
Baking Time: 45 minutes
Cooling Time: 2 hours

Under 125 calories per serving
Approximately 20 grams carbohydrate per serving

SWEET POTATO BALLS

Serves 40

10 sweet potatoes
2 tablespoons sesame tahini
1 teaspoon vanilla
2 tablespoons frozen apple or orange juice concentrate, thawed
¼ cup chestnut flour
2 eggs beaten with one tablespoon apple juice
1 cup fine sugarless cake or cookie crumbs
Oil for frying
1 cup ground almonds or sesame seeds

Preparation Time: 50 minutes
Chilling Time: 1 hour
Frying Time: 20 minutes

Preheat oven to 400 degrees and bake yams in their jackets until soft. Peel and mash. Mix in tahini, vanilla, juice concentrate and chestnut flour. Chill mixture for 1 hour. Shape into teaspoon-size balls. Roll in egg mixture and then in cookie or cake crumbs. Heat 2 inches of oil for frying. Fry several balls at a time until golden and crisp. Roll in ground almonds or sesame seeds. Serve while warm.

Approximately 225 calories per serving
Under 30 grams carbohydrate per serving

ORANGE, PUMPKIN, CURRANT PIE

Serves 8

½ Flaky Pastry Dough recipe (see p. 16)

FILLING INGREDIENTS
2 cups pumpkin purée (see p. 146)
4 eggs, beaten
1 cup milk

Preheat oven to 425 degrees. Roll pastry into a 12-inch circle. Line a 9-inch pie plate, trim and flute edges.

In a bowl, mix pumpkin purée, eggs, milk, milk powder, soy flour, juice concentrate and orange peel. Pour into pie shell. Bake for 10 minutes at 450. Reduce heat to 350 and bake 35 minutes longer until firm.

2 tablespoons non-instant skim
milk powder
1 tablespoon soy flour
½ cup frozen orange juice concentrate, thawed
1 teaspoon cinnamon
2 teaspoons grated orange peel

ORANGE, CURRANT GLAZE IN-
GREDIENTS
1½ cups orange juice
½ cup currants
1 teaspoon grated orange peel
5 teaspoons cornstarch

Preparation Time: 20 minutes
Baking Time: 45 minutes
Chilling and Assembling Time: 3
hours

While pie bakes, prepare glaze. In a saucepan, combine orange juice, currants, orange peel and cornstarch. Cook over medium heat, stirring occasionally, until mixture thickens. Spread mixture carefully over pie. Refrigerate for 2 to 3 hours before serving.

Approximately 150 calories per serving
Approximately 30 grams carbohydrate per serving

CRANBERRY CHEESE MOLD

Serves 8

1 envelope unflavored gelatin
¼ cup frozen apple juice concentrate, thawed
1 cup whole fresh cranberries
1½ cups apple juice
1 cup part-skim milk ricotta
cheese
1 teaspoon vanilla

Stir gelatin into apple juice concentrate and set aside. In a saucepan, combine cranberries and apple juice. Cook until cranberries begin to pop, then mash them. Stir in gelatin mixture. Chill for 1 hour until mixture resembles the consistency of custard but is not set. In an electric blender, blend ricotta and vanilla until smooth. Fold ricotta mixture into partially jelled cranberry mixture. Fold in orange wedges. Pour into a 4-cup gelatin mold. Chill for 3 hours or until firm. Unmold and surround with orange slices.

2 oranges, peeled with membranes removed, cut in wedges

1 orange, cut in half and thinly sliced, for garnish

Preparation Time: 15 minutes
Chilling Time: 4 hours

Approximately 150 calories per serving
Approximately 30 grams carbohydrate per serving

PUMPKIN BREAD

Serves 15 to 20

4 eggs
1 cup apple juice
¼ cup liquid barley malt
2 cups pumpkin purée (see p. 146)
1¼ cups whole wheat pastry flour
1½ cups brown rice flour
¼ cup soy flour
2 teaspoons baking powder
1 teaspoon cinnamon
½ teaspoon ground cloves
½ cup chopped dates
½ cup walnut pieces

Preheat oven to 350 degrees. In a bowl, beat eggs, apple juice, liquid barley malt and pumpkin purée. In a separate bowl, mix pastry flour, rice flour, soy flour, baking powder, cinnamon and cloves with a wire whisk. Gradually stir dry mixture into liquids to form a smooth batter. Stir in dates and walnuts. Pour batter into 2 loaf pans and bake for 1¼ hours until a knife inserted into the center comes out clean.

To use as a hostess gift, wrap loaves in colored cellophane or place in decorative tins.

Preparation Time: 10 minutes
Baking Time: 1 hour 15 minutes

Under 150 calories per serving
Approximately 30 grams carbohydrate per serving

CRANBERRY BREAD

Serves 10 to 12

3 eggs
¼ cup oil
½ cup apple juice
¼ cup liquid barley malt
2 tablespoons frozen orange
  juice concentrate, thawed
2 tablespoons frozen apple
  juice concentrate, thawed
1 tablespoon grated orange peel
1 cup whole wheat pastry flour
1 cup brown rice flour
2 teaspoons baking powder
1 cup whole fresh cranberries
½ cup chopped walnuts

Preparation Time: 10 minutes
Baking Time: 1 hour

Preheat oven to 350 degrees. In a bowl, beat eggs, oil, apple juice, malt, orange juice concentrate, apple juice concentrate and grated orange peel. In a separate bowl, mix pastry flour, rice flour and baking powder with a wire whisk. Gradually stir dry mixture into liquid ingredients to form a smooth batter. Fold in cranberries and walnuts. Pour into an oiled loaf pan and bake 1 hour until a knife inserted into the center comes out clean.

Cranberry bread makes a delicious gift when placed in a decorative rectangular tin or wrapped in colored foil.

Approximately 225 calories per serving
Over 35 grams carbohydrate per serving

CRANBERRY COFFEE RING

Serves 24 (Makes 2 coffee rings)

DOUGH INGREDIENTS
2 cups warm apple juice
½ cup frozen apple juice concentrate, thawed
2 tablespoons oil
2 tablespoons baking yeast
2 eggs, beaten
4½ cups whole wheat pastry
  flour
1½ cups soy flour

To make coffee bread dough, combine warm apple juice, apple juice concentrate and oil. Sprinkle yeast over liquid. Allow to stand 10 minutes until yeast dissolves. Beat in eggs. In a separate bowl, mix pastry flour, soy flour, gluten flour and cardamom with a wire whisk. Beat 2 cups of flour mixture into yeast mixture. Cover, place in a warm spot and allow to stand for 20 minutes until a sponge forms. Beat in remaining flour mixture to form a soft dough. If dough is sticky, knead in additional whole wheat pastry flour. Knead on a

1½ cups gluten flour
2 teaspoons cardamom

FILLING INGREDIENTS
2 cups whole fresh cranberries
1 cup apple juice
3 tablespoons frozen apple
  juice concentrate, thawed
⅓ cup raisins or currants
2 tablespoons cornstarch or arrowroot starch dissolved in 2
  tablespoons water
2 egg yolks, beaten

FROSTING INGREDIENTS
¼ cup soft unsalted butter
1½ cups non-instant skim milk
  powder
¾ cup apple juice
1 teaspoon vanilla
3 tablespoons chopped walnuts

Preparation Time: 3 hours
Baking Time: 35 minutes
Frosting Time: 5 minutes

floured board for 10 minutes until smooth and elastic. Place in an oiled bowl, cover and let rise for 1½ hours.

Divide dough in half and roll into two 12 x 20-inch rectangles. Cover with a towel and prepare filling.

In a saucepan, combine cranberries, apple juice, apple juice concentrate and raisins or currants. Cook over medium-high heat, bringing to a gentle boil. When cranberries begin to pop, stir in starch-and-water paste. Continue stirring until mixture thickens. Remove from heat. Cool to lukewarm and spread evenly over rectangles of dough. Roll each in jelly roll fashion. Bring ends together to form two circles and seal edges. Cover and allow to rise in a warm place until doubled in bulk, about 1 hour. Preheat oven to 350 degrees. Brush rings with egg yolks and bake for 35 minutes until golden brown.

To make frosting, blend butter, milk powder, apple juice and vanilla in a blender or food processor until smooth. Frost rings while warm and sprinkle with nuts. Cool.

Wrapped in colored cellophane or placed in decorative cake tins these coffee breads make delicious gifts. They can also be wrapped in foil and reheated before serving.

Approximately 150 calories per serving
Approximately 30 grams carbohydrate per serving

PRUNE BUNDT CAKE
Serves 16 to 18

BATTER INGREDIENTS
1¼ cups boiling apple juice
1½ cups chopped prunes
1 tablespoon grated lemon peel
⅓ cup oil
⅓ cup liquid barley malt
1 teaspoon baking soda
5 eggs, separated
2 teaspoons vanilla
1⅓ cups whole wheat pastry
  flour
1⅓ cups brown rice flour
¼ cup non-instant skim milk
  powder
1 teaspoon baking powder

PRUNE GLAZE INGREDIENTS
1 cup prune juice
2 tablespoons cornstarch
1 teaspoon vanilla
¼ cup chopped walnuts

Preparation Time: 50 minutes
Baking Time: 90 minutes

Preheat oven to 350 degrees. Pour boiling apple juice over prunes and lemon peel. Let stand 30 minutes. Drain prunes, reserving liquid in a large bowl. Beat oil, malt, baking soda, egg yolks and vanilla into reserved liquid. In a separate bowl, mix pastry flour, rice flour, milk powder and baking powder with a wire whisk. Gradually stir dry mixture into liquids to form a smooth batter. Stir in prunes. Beat egg whites until stiff and fold into batter. Oil and dust a bundt pan. Pour batter into pan and bake for 90 minutes until a toothpick inserted into the center comes out clean. Cool for 10 minutes and turn onto a plate to cool.

To make glaze, combine prune juice, cornstarch, vanilla and walnuts in a saucepan, heat, stirring occasionally, until mixture thickens. Drizzle over cake while still warm. Allow to cool.

Bundt cake makes a welcome gift if placed in a decorative tin.

Approximately 225 calories per serving
Over 35 grams carbohydrate per serving

ZUCCHINI BREAD
Serves 10 to 15

¼ cup oil
¾ cup apple juice
1 cup grated unpeeled zucchini
1 tablespoon grated lemon peel

Preheat oven to 350 degrees. In a bowl, beat oil, apple juice, zucchini, lemon peel, liquid barley malt and eggs with a wooden spoon. In a separate bowl, mix pastry flour, rice flour, baking powder, soy flour and cinna-

¼ cup liquid barley malt
3 eggs, beaten
1 cup whole wheat pastry flour
1 cup brown rice flour
2 teaspoons baking powder
2 tablespoons soy flour
1 teaspoon cinnamon
⅓ cup chopped walnuts

Preparation Time: 10 minutes
Baking Time: 1 hour

mon. Stir dry ingredients gradually into liquids to form a smooth batter. Stir in chopped nuts. Pour into an oiled loaf pan and bake for 1 hour until a knife inserted into the center comes out clean. Remove from pan and cool.

As a gift, zucchini bread can be wrapped in cellophane or colored foil and decorated with a bow.

Approximately 225 calories per serving
Over 35 grams carbohydrate per serving

CARROT CAKE

Serves 9

CAKE INGREDIENTS
2 tablespoons oil
2 cups grated carrots
3 eggs, beaten
¼ cup apple butter
1 cup apple cider
¼ cup liquid barley malt
1 cup whole wheat pastry flour
1 cup brown rice flour
½ cup raw wheat germ
2 teaspoons baking powder
1 teaspoon cinnamon
½ teaspoon ground cloves
¼ cup tahini
2 tablespoons frozen orange
   juice concentrate, thawed
2 teaspoons grated orange peel
⅓ cup raisins or currants

Preheat oven to 350 degrees. In a heavy frying pan heat oil. Stir in grated carrots and sauté for 10 minutes. Pour into a mixing bowl and cool. With a wooden spoon, mix in eggs, apple butter, cider and malt. In a separate bowl, mix pastry flour, brown rice flour, raw wheat germ, baking powder, cinnamon and cloves with a wire whisk. With a pastry blender or fork cut tahini into flour mixture to form a coarse meal. Stir in orange juice concentrate and orange peel. Gradually stir in liquid mixture. Add raisins or currants. Pour batter into an oiled 9-inch square baking pan and bake for 50 minutes or until a knife inserted into the center comes out clean. Cool for 10 minutes, remove from pan and cool on a wire rack.

To make frosting, blend soft butter, milk powder, apple juice, orange peel and vanilla in an electric blender or food processor until smooth and thick. Frost cake.

FROSTING INGREDIENTS

2 tablespoons soft unsalted butter

¾ cup non-instant milk powder

½ cup apple juice

1 teaspoon grated orange peel

½ teaspoon vanilla

Preparation Time: 20 minutes
Baking Time: 50 minutes

This cake makes a welcome gift if placed in a square tin or decorative box.

Approximately 225 calories per serving
Over 35 grams carbohydrate per serving

APPLESAUCE BUNDT CAKE

Serves 20

CAKE INGREDIENTS

⅓ cup oil

2 cups unsweetened applesauce

6 eggs, separated

⅓ cup apple juice

⅓ cup liquid barley malt

1⅓ cups whole wheat pastry flour

1⅓ cups brown rice flour

⅓ cup non-instant skim milk powder

2 teaspoons baking powder

1 teaspoon cinnamon

1 tablespoon grated orange peel

Preheat oven to 350 degrees. In a bowl, beat oil, applesauce, egg yolks, apple juice and barley malt. In a separate bowl, mix pastry flour, rice flour, milk powder, baking powder and cinnamon with a wire whisk. Gradually beat dry ingredients into liquids to form a smooth batter. Stir in orange peel. Beat egg whites until stiff. Fold into batter. Pour into an oiled and dusted bundt pan and bake for 90 minutes until a knife inserted into the center comes out clean. Remove from pan to cool.

To make frosting, beat tahini, apple cider, cinnamon and starch in a saucepan. Heat, stirring occasionally, until thickened. Cool to lukewarm and drizzle over bundt cake.

As a gift, place in a decorative tin or box.

FROSTING INGREDIENTS
2 teaspoons sesame tahini
1 cup apple cider
½ teaspoon cinnamon
5 teaspoons cornstarch

Preparation Time: 20 minutes
Baking Time: 90 minutes

Approximately 225 calories per serving
Over 35 grams carbohydrate per serving

CHESTNUT KNOTS

Serves 12 to 16

3 cups fresh chestnuts
2 cups water
1 cup apple juice
Flaky Pastry Dough recipe (see
   p. 16)
2 egg yolks, beaten

With a sharp knife slit chestnuts. Boil in water for 20 minutes. Remove skins and discard water. Place chestnuts in apple juice and boil until tender. Purée in an electric blender or food processor until smooth and thick.

Roll pastry dough into a rectangle and cut into 4-inch squares. Spread chestnut purée thinly on each square and roll up in jelly roll fashion. Cross the ends of each roll over one another to form a loose knot, and place on an oiled baking sheet. Heat oven to 375 degrees. Brush knots with egg yolk and bake for 25 minutes until lightly browned. Cool.

These pastries make a delicious gift if placed in a decorative box or cookie tin.

Preparation Time: 1 hour
Baking Time: 25 minutes

Under 150 calories per serving
Under 30 grams carbohydrate per serving

RAISIN CHESTNUT STRUDEL

Serves 16 (Makes 2 strudels)

5 cups fresh chestnuts
4 cups water
2 cups apple cider
⅔ cup raisins
2 tablespoons grated orange peel
½ Strudel Dough recipe (see p. 17)

With a sharp knife, slit chestnuts. Place chestnuts and water in a pan and boil for 20 minutes. Drain and peel chestnuts of inner and outer skins. Place peeled chestnuts, apple cider and raisins in a covered pot and boil gently until chestnuts are soft. Add orange peel and blend to a purée in an electric blender or food processor.

Roll strudel dough according to directions on p. 17 and divide in half. Fill each with chestnut filling and bake for 45 minutes until crisp and golden brown. Cool.

Wrap strudels in colored aluminum foil as a Thanksgiving gift.

Preparation Time: 1 hour
Baking Time: 45 minutes

Approximately 225 calories per serving
Approximately 30 grams carbohydrate per serving

APPLE-FILLED DOUGHNUTS

Serves 24

DOUGH INGREDIENTS
1 tablespoon baking yeast
¾ cup warm apple juice
3 tablespoons frozen apple juice concentrate, thawed
2 tablespoons oil
½ cup orange juice
1 tablespoon grated orange peel
3½ cups whole wheat pastry flour
4 tablespoons gluten flour

To make dough, sprinkle yeast over warm apple juice and allow to stand until dissolved. Stir in apple juice concentrate, oil, orange juice and orange peel. In a separate bowl, mix whole wheat flour and gluten flour with a wire whisk until well combined. Beat 1½ cups of flour mixture into liquids. Set in a warm place for 20 minutes until a sponge forms. With a wooden spoon beat in remaining flour to form a soft dough. Knead on a floured board until smooth and elastic. If dough becomes sticky, knead in additional pastry flour. Place in a covered bowl and refrigerate for 1 hour until thoroughly chilled.

FILLING INGREDIENTS

2 cups finely chopped unpeeled apples

2 tablespoons frozen apple juice concentrate, thawed

1 tablespoon cornstarch or arrowroot starch

1 teaspoon cinnamon

Oil for frying

GLAZE INGREDIENTS

2 tablespoons soft unsalted butter

¾ cup non-instant skim milk powder

1 tablespoon apple butter

½ teaspoon cinnamon

½ cup apple juice

Preparation Time: 2 hours
Frying Time: 25 minutes

While dough chills prepare filling. Combine apples, apple juice concentrate, cornstarch and cinnamon in a saucepan. Heat over low heat, stirring occasionally, until a chunky applesauce forms. Remove from heat.

Roll chilled dough ¼ inch thick. Cut into circles with English muffin rings or a tuna can. Place 1 tablespoon of filling in the center of half of the circles. Cover with the second half of circles and seal edges with moistened fingers. Place on an oiled baking sheet, and cover. Set in a warm place to rise until doubled in bulk, about 1 hour.

Heat 4 inches of oil to a gentle boil. Fry doughnuts on both sides until lightly browned and fully cooked. Drain on paper towels.

To make glaze, blend soft butter, milk powder, apple butter, cinnamon and apple juice until smooth. Frost doughnuts.

Placed in decorative boxes or tins, doughnuts make delicious gifts. Doughnuts may be reheated at 300 degrees before serving for a just-fried taste.

Over 250 calories per serving
Over 35 grams carbohydrate per serving

SWEET CROISSANTS

Serves 36

2 tablespoons baking yeast

2 cups warm apple juice

3 tablespoons melted unsalted butter

2 eggs, beaten

⅓ cup frozen apple juice concentrate, thawed

Sprinkle baking yeast over warm apple juice. Let stand for 10 minutes until yeast dissolves. Stir in melted butter, eggs, and apple juice concentrate. In a separate bowl, mix whole wheat pastry flour, soy flour and gluten flour with a wire whisk. Beat 2 cups of flour mixture into liquids, cover and set in a warm place for 20 minutes to form a sponge. With a wooden spoon

4½ cups whole wheat pastry
flour
1½ cups soy flour
1½ cups gluten flour

½ cup melted unsalted butter
1 cup chopped walnuts or
pecans

⅓ cup frozen apple juice concentrate, thawed, beaten with
1 egg

beat in remaining flour mixture. Turn onto a floured board and knead for 10 minutes until smooth and elastic. If dough becomes sticky, knead in additional flour. Cover, and set in a warm place to rise for 1½ hours. Divide into two portions and roll into two squares ⅛-inch thick. Brush with melted butter and sprinkle with nuts. Cut into 4-inch squares. Cut each square in half diagonally to form triangles. Roll each triangle from the long edge toward the point in jelly roll fashion. Place rolls on oiled baking sheets 2 inches apart, cover, set in a warm place and let rise until doubled in bulk, about 1 hour.

Preheat oven to 350 degrees. Brush rolls with apple juice concentrate and egg mixture. Bake for 25 minutes until lightly browned.

Placed in decorative tins or boxes these croissants make delicious gifts, and they can be reheated at 300 degrees for a fresh-baked taste.

Preparation Time: 3 to 4 hours
Baking Time: 25 minutes

Approximately 225 calories per serving
Over 35 grams carbohydrate per serving

HOT APPLE CRANBERRY PUNCH
Serves 12 to 16

2 cups whole fresh cranberries
4 cups apple juice
3 tablespoons frozen apple
juice concentrate, thawed
1 apple, unpeeled, cored and
thinly sliced
1 teaspoon lemon juice

In a pot, heat cranberries, apple juice and apple juice concentrate until cranberries begin to pop. Sieve to remove cranberry peels. Toss apple in lemon juice to prevent discoloring. Pour punch into a punch bowl, and float apple slices on top.

Preparation and Cooking Time:
20 minutes

Under 150 calories per serving
Under 30 grams carbohydrate per serving

HOT ORANGE CINNAMON DRINK

Serves 4 to 6

1 quart orange juice
½ teaspoon cinnamon
4 to 6 3-inch cinnamon sticks
4 to 6 orange slices

Heat orange juice and cinnamon. Pour into mugs or cups. Insert cinnamon sticks and cut a slit in orange slices and place on edge of cup.

Preparation and Cooking Time:
10 minutes

Under 150 calories per serving
Approximately 25 grams carbohydrate per serving

RAISIN TURMERIC MILK

Serves 4 to 6

1 quart milk
1 teaspoon turmeric
3 tablespoons raisins

In a pot, combine milk, turmeric and raisins. Heat over low heat for 10 minutes or until flavors of raisins and turmeric are well combined. Pour into glasses and serve.

Preparation and Cooking Time:
10 minutes

Under 150 calories per serving
Approximately 20 grams carbohydrate per serving

Index

Airola, Paavo, 7
Allspice, 5
Almond:
  coconut cream eggs, 112
  crunch, 77
  drops, 41–42
  lemon, sandwich crème cookies,
    39–40
  plums in pastry, 132
  sauce, fancy baked bananas with,
    55
  sweet stuffed pumpkin, 143
  tarts, Swedish, 58
Almond extract, 5
Angels, milk ball, 50
Apple(s):
  applesauce:
    Bundt cake, 177–78
    cranberry, baked cranberry
      apple dumplings with, 162–63
    mousse, 56
    pie, yam, 165
  butter, 36
    custard, 153
    doughnuts, 100
  caramel, 158
    peanut butter, 159
  carob coconut candied, 160
  Charlotte, baked, 24

cheese bread pudding, Christmas,
  25
cranberry:
  dumplings, baked, with cran-
    berry applesauce, 162–63
  nut pie, 169
  punch, hot, 181
  -filled doughnuts, 179–80
  fritters with sesame sauce, 164
  gift-wrapped, with vanilla sauce,
    22
  ginger pudding, New Year's, 62
  Halloween compote, 144–45
  Indian pudding, 166
  pie:
    chestnut, 169
    cranberry nut, 169
    mince crumb, 30
    "mincemeat," 168
  plum cobbler, 26
  prune strudel, 60
  rings, French fried, 165
  sherry, mousse, 56–57
  snow, 52
  soufflés, individual, 29
  turnovers with cardamom sauce,
    59
Apple juice, 5, 10
  calories in, 5–6

Apple juice (*cont.*)
  concentrate, 5, 6, 10
  red, white and blue gelatin,
    139
  striped popsicles, 140
Apricot soufflé, baked, 94
Aquavit, Swedish glogg, 46
Avocado sherbet with pineapple
    sauce, simple, 115

Baby walnut date tarts, 37
Baking powder, 12–13
Bamboo, 11
Banana(s):
  with almond sauce, fancy baked,
    55
  cranberry, cream delight, 55–56
  crêpes, 92
  pudding with cranberry sauce,
    steamed, 34–35
  sherbet with hot carob sauce, easy,
    114
  and sweet potato casserole, 144
Barley malt. *See* Malt, liquid barley
Berry zabaglione, 124
  see also Blueberry(ies); Rasp-
    berry(ies); Strawberry(ies)
Beverages. *See specific types of bever-
    ages, e.g.* Eggnog; Punch
Big popcorn bunny, 110
Black Forest cake, 68–69
Blackstrap molasses, 5, 11
Blintzes:
  Eastern breakfast, 91
  Hanukkah dessert, 33–34
Blueberry(ies):
  bread, 128

cupcakes, 130
flag cake, 138–139
pie:
  glazed, 119
  red, white and blue, 136–37
red, white and blue gelatin, 139
striped popsicles, 140
strudel, 127
unsweetened frozen, 10
zabaglione, 124
Bonbons, cream cheese nut, 82
Bread(s):
  blueberry, 128
  cranberry, 173
    coffee ring, 173–74
  dessert. *See* Dessert breads
  Eastern, 104–105
  pineapple, 103
  pudding, Christmas apple cheese,
    25
  pumpkin, 172
  rolls, orange cinnamon, 103–104
  zucchini, 175–76
Brown rice flour, 12
Bundt cake:
  applesauce, 177
  prune, 175
Buns, hot cross, 107
Burry's Health Food Carob Bars,
    11
Butter:
  apple, 36
    doughnuts, 100
  buttery snowballs, 63
  unsalted, 12

Café au lait, meringue, 109
Cafix, 11

Cake:
applesauce Bundt, 177–78
Black Forest, 68–69
Bundt:
applesauce, 177
prune, 175
carob:
cheesecake, 58–59
Valentine's, 70–71
carrot, 176–77
cheesecake:
carob, 58–59
cranberry Christmas, 27
creamy apple walnut, 58
orange, 152
cupcakes. *See* Cupcakes
flag, 138–39
fruit, 42–43
fresh, and custard roll, 129
molasses marble, with lemon
sauce, 89–90
orange:
cheesecake, 152
open face, 151–52
peaches and cream, 121
pumpkin, 149–50
strawberry, 124–25
shortcake, 122
sweet potato, with raisin sauce,
150–51
techniques for whole grain, 8
Calories, cutting, with naturally sweet
desserts, 5–6
Candy:
almond:
coconut cream eggs, 112
crunch, 77
caramel(s):
cream, 79
Easter characters, 111
nut-coated, 77
pecan clusters, 80
pops, head-shaped, 85
cashew eggs, chewy, 111
coconut:
chews, carob capped, 78
chews, molasses, 78
cream eggs, almond, 112
mint carob log, 81
mocha balls, 83
nut:
bonbons, cream cheese, 88
-coated caramels, 77
English toffee, 82
orange balls, Halloween, 154
popcorn:
bunny, big, 109
fudge, 154
pralines, 81
raisin sesame clusters, 79
toffee:
English, 82
layered peanut butter carob, 76
walnuts, glazed, 80
Cantaloupe. *See* Melon(s)
Caramel(s):
apples, 158
peanut butter, 159
cream, 79
Easter characters, 111
nut-coated, 77
pecan clusters, 80
pops, heart-shaped, 85
pumpkin flan, 162

Carbohydrates, 6–7
  unrefined, 7
Cardamom, 5
  sauce, apple turnovers with, 59
  Swedish glogg, 46
Caro, 11
Carob, 5, 6, 11–12
  cake:
    cheesecake, 58–59
    cheesecake, refrigerator, 71
    Valentine's, 70–71
  chiffon pie, 72
  coconut:
    candied apples, 160
    capped, chews, 78
    cookies, 36
  cold, 135
  fancy mocha, 109
  fondue, 67
  log, mint, 81
  mint:
    layered dessert, 95–96
    log, 81
    sandwich cookies, 40
  mousse, 73
  parfaits, strawberry, 74
  peanut wafers, 62–63
  sauce:
    easy banana sherbet with hot,
      114
    strawberry profiteroles with,
      67–68
  strawberry(ies):
    cheese roll, 69–70
    frozen, 85
    parfaits, 74
    profiteroles with, sauce, 67–
      68

  toffee, layered peanut butter,
    76
  torte, German, 61
Carrot:
  cake, 176–77
  cookies, 155
  pudding, 147
Cashew eggs, chewy, 111
Charlotte, baked apple, 24
Cheese:
  bread pudding, Christmas apple,
    25
  cheesecake:
    carob, 58–59
    carob, refrigerator, 71
    cranberry Christmas, 27
    creamy apple walnut, 58
    orange, 152
  cottage cheese. See Cottage cheese
  cream. See Cream cheese
  mold, cranberry, 171–72
  ricotta. See Ricotta cheese, skim
    milk
  roll, carob strawberry, 69–70
  -stuffed pears, 53
Cherry(ies):
  Black Forest cake, 68–69
  unsweetened canned, 10
  unsweetened frozen, 10
Chestnut(s), 7
  Halloween compote, 144–45
  knots, 178
  pie, apple, 169
  sauce, plum pie with, 25–26
  strudel, raisin, 179
Chewy cashew eggs, 111
Chiffon pie:
  carob, 72

Chiffon pie (*cont.*)
  pineapple, 97
  strawberry, 72–73, 118
Children, holiday snacks for, 8
  Christmas or Hanukkah, 47–50
  Easter, 110–12
  Fourth of July, 136–40
  Halloween, 158–60
  Valentine's day, 84–86
Christmas-Hanukkah treats, 21–50
  almond(s):
    drops, 41–42
    lemon, sandwich crème cookies,
      39–40
  apple(s):
    baked, Charlotte, 24
    butter, 36
    cheese bread pudding,
      Christmas, 25
    gift-wrapped, with vanilla sauce,
      22
    mince crumb pie, 30
    plum cobbler, 26
    soufflés, individual, 29
  banana pudding with cranberry
    sauce, steamed, 34–35
  blintzes, Hanukkah, 33–34
  carob:
    coconut cookies, 36
    mint sandwich cookies, 40
  for children, 47–50
    Christmas canes, 49
    cutout ginger cookies, 50
    gingerbread characters, 47
    milk ball angels, 50
    sweet dough figures, 48
  cider, mulled, 46
  cranberry:
    Christmas cheesecake, 27

    Christmas pie, 28
    sauce, steamed banana pudding
      with, 34–35
  cream puff Christmas tree, 23
  date(s):
    baby walnut, tarts, 37
    -filled cookies, 41
    stuffed, 35
  floating islands, 29
  fruit cake, 42–43
  joe froggers, 38–39
  latkes, dessert, 33
  lemon almond sandwich crème
    cookies, 39–40
  orange cookies, delicate, 42
  pinwheels, 38
  plum(s):
    apple, cobbler, 26
    pie with chestnut sauce, 25–
      26
    pudding, English, 44–45
    stuffed, 35
    tapioca, parfaits, 30–31
  raisin nut mousse, 28
  sherried macaroon balls, 37
  Swedish glogg, 46
  Swedish tea ring, 43–44
  trifle, English Christmas, 31–32
  wine, spiced, 45
  yogurt cheese pancakes, Hanuk-
    kah, 32
Christmas tree, cream puff, 23
Cider, mulled, 46
Cinnamon, 5
  mulled cider, 46
  orange drink, hot, 182
  rolls, orange, 103–104
  spiced wine, 45

Cloves:
  mulled cider, 46
  spiced wine, 45
Cocoa, 6
Coconut:
  buttery snowballs, 63
  carob:
    candied apples, 160
    capped, chews, 78
    cookies, 36
  chews:
    carob capped, 78
    molasses, 78
  cream eggs, almond, 112
  milk ball angels, 50
  orange haystacks, 156
  peach cupcakes, 131
  piña colada meringue pie, 95
  sherried macaroon balls, 37
  unsweetened shredded, 5
Coconut juice, piña colada punch, 136
Coffee ring, cranberry, 173–74
Coffee substitutes, grain, 11
  coffee jelly, 97
  cold mocha, 135
  fancy mocha, 109
  meringue café au lait, 109
  mocha balls, 83
  tahini, walnut parfaits, 166–67
Cold carob, 135
Cold mocha, 135
Confectioner's sugar, 6
Cookies:
  almond drops, 41–42
  carob:
    coconut, 36
    mint sandwich, 40

carrot, 155
date-filled, 41
ginger, cutout, 50
gingerbread characters, 47
lemon almond sandwich crème, 39–40
milk ball angels, 50
orange, delicate, 42
pumpkin, 155–56
sweet dough figures, 48
Corn. *See* Popcorn
Cornmeal, Indian pudding, 166
Corn syrup, 4
Cottage cheese:
  blintzes, Hanukkah dessert, 33–34
  cheesecake:
    carob, 58–59
    carob, refrigerator, 71
    orange, 152
  yogurt cheese pancakes, Hanukkah, 32
Cranberry:
  apple:
    dumplings, baked, with cranberry applesauce, 162–63
    nut pie, 169
    punch, hot, 181
  banana cream delight, 55–56
  bread, 173
  cheese mold, 171–72
  Christmas cheesecake, 27
  Christmas pie, 28
  coffee ring, 173–74
  orange:
    mold, 163–64
    torte, 148–49
  sauce, steamed banana pudding with, 34–35

Cream:
    caramels, 79
    cranberry banana, delight, 55–56
    creamy apple walnut cheesecake,
      57
    orange Bavarian, 143–44
    peaches and, cake, 121
    pie, raspberry, 126–27
    pineapple soufflé, 92
    strawberry:
      hot milk, 86
      ice cream parfaits, 116
      Romanoff, 123
      shortcake, 122
    whipped, 6
Cream cheese, 6
    almond coconut cream eggs, 112
    creamy apple walnut cheesecake,
      57
    nut bonbons, 82
    strawberry cream gelatin, 120
Cream puff(s):
    Christmas tree, 23
    orange, 156–57
    pastry, 19
      techniques for whole grain, 9
Creamy apple walnut cheesecake, 57
Crème de menthe, 11
    mint carob log, 81
    soufflé, 93–94
Crêpes:
    banana, 92
    eggless, low calorie, 18
    strawberry, 75–76
    Suzette, 91
    whole wheat, delicate, 18
    see also Blintzes
Croissants, sweet, 180–81

Crumble crust, 17
Crust, crumble, 17
Cupcakes:
    blueberry, 130
    peach coconut, 131
Currants:
    English plum pudding, 44–45
    orange, pumpkin pie, 170–71
    sweet stuffed pumpkin, 143
Custard:
    apple butter, 153
    for éclairs, 99–100
    for floating islands, 29
    fresh fruit and, roll, 129
    for red, white and blue pie,
      136–37
    for tahini, walnut, coffee parfaits,
      166–67
Cutout ginger cookies, 50

Date(s):
    apple mince crumb pie, 30
    -filled cookies, 41
    stuffed, 35
    tarts, baby walnut, 37
Delicate orange cookies, 42
Delicate whole wheat crêpes, 18
Dessert blintzes, Hanukkah, 33–
    34
Dessert breads, techniques for whole
    grain, 8–9
Dessert latkes, 33
Diabetics, 6–7
Dough, pastry. *See* Pastry dough
Doughnuts:
    apple butter, 100
    apple-filled, 179–80
    lemon, 101

Easter recipes, 87–112
  apricot soufflé, baked, 94
  banana crêpes, 92
  blintzes, breakfast, 91
  children's Easter treats, 110–12
    almond coconut cream eggs,
      112
    big popcorn bunny, 110
    caramel Easter characters, 111
    chewy cashew eggs, 111
    pastel punch, 112
  coffee jelly, 97
  crème de menthe soufflé, 93–94
  crêpes:
    banana, 92
    Suzette, 91
  doughnuts:
    apple butter, 100
    lemon, 101
  Easter bread, 104–105
  éclairs, 99–100
  grapefruit, broiled, 98
  hot cross buns, 107
  jelly roll, old-fashioned, 99
  lemon:
    doughnuts, 101
    loaf, 102
    sauce, molasses marble cake
      with, 89–90
  meringue:
    café au lait, 109
    mushrooms, 106
  mint carob layered dessert, 95–96
  mocha, fancy, 109
  molasses marble cake with lemon
    sauce, 89–90
  nut-filled horns, 105–106
  orange:
    baked soufflé, 93

  Bavarian, 96
  cinammon rolls, 103–104
  piña colada meringue pie, 95
  pineapple:
    bread, 103
    chiffon pie, 97
    parfaits, 98
    rice, glorified, 90
    soufflé, 92
    tea rings, 108
Easy banana sherbet with hot carob
    sauce, 114
Éclairs, 99–100
Egg(s), 8
  apple butter custard, 153
  carrot pudding, 147
  chiffon pie:
    carob, 72
    strawberry, 72–73
  eggnog:
    strawberry, 83
    summer, 134
  floating islands, 29
  yam pudding, 153
  see also Meringue(s); Soufflé(s)
Eggnog:
  strawberry, 83
  summer, 134
English Christmas trifle, 31–32
English plum pudding, 44–45
English toffee, 82

Fancy baked bananas with almond
    sauce, 55
Fancy mocha, 109
Fiber, foods high in, 7
Flag cake, 138–39
Flaky pastry dough, 16

Flan, caramel pumpkin, 162
Floating islands, 29
Flour, white, 8
Flours, whole grain. *See* Whole
    grains; *specific flours, e.g.* Glu-
    ten flour; Soy flour
Fondue, carob, 67
Fourth of July desserts, 113–40
    avocado sherbet with pineapple
        sauce, simple, 115
    banana sherbet with hot carob
        sauce, easy, 114
    blueberry:
        bread, 128
        cupcakes, 130
        pie, glazed, 119
        zabaglione, 124
    for children, 136–40
        flag cake, 138–39
        patriotic soda, 140
        red, white and blue gelatin, 139
        red, white and blue pie, 136–
            37
        striped popsicles, 140
    cold carob, 135
    cold mocha, 135
    eggnog, summer, 134
    fruit:
        fresh, and custard roll, 129
        fresh, logs, 133–34
        jelled sherried, 116
        summer eggnog, 134
    grape mousse, 117
    melons:
        pastel parfaits, 117–18
        sherbet-stuffed, 115
        watermelon gelatin, 120
    pastel parfaits, 117–18

peach(es):
    coconut cupcakes, 131
    and cream cake, 121
    fresh baked, 122–23
    pie, glazed, 119
    soufflé, fresh, 120–21
persimmon sherbet, 114
pineapple sauce, simple avocado
    sherbet with, 115
plums in pastry, 132
punch:
    piña colada, 136
    sparkling pink, 136
raspberry:
    cream pie, 126–27
    zabaglione, 124
strawberry:
    cake, 124–25
    chiffon pie, 118
    cream gelatin, 120
    ice cream parfaits, 116
    ricotta pie, 126
    Romanoff, 123
    shortcake, 122
    sparkling pink punch, 136
    strudel, 127
    tarts, glazed, 132–33
    turnovers, 125
    zabaglione, 124
    watermelon gelatin, 120
French fried apple rings, 165
Fresh baked peaches, 122–23
Fresh fruit and custard roll,
    129
Fresh fruit logs, 133–34
Fresh peach soufflé, 120–21
Fritters with sesame sauce, apple,
    164

Frosting, 6
  see also specific cake and pastry recipes
Frozen carob strawberries, 85
Fructose, 7
Fruit(s), 7
  cake, 42–43
  carob fondue, 67
  dried, 5
  English Christmas trifle, 31–32
  fresh, 5
    and custard roll, 129
    logs, 133–34
  Halloween compote, 144–45
  jelled sherried, 116
  soup, Swedish, 53
    unsweetened canned, 10
    unsweetened frozen, 10
    winter, compote in wine sauce, 54
    see also Fruit concentrates, frozen; Fruit juices; *specific fruits*
Fruit concentrates, frozen, 5
  see also specific frozen fruit concentrates
Fruit juices, 4–5, 7
  see also specific fruit juices
Fudge, popcorn, 154

Gelatin:
  orange:
    Bavarian, 96, 143–44
    cranberry mold, 163–64
  red, white and blue, 139
  strawberry cream, 120
  watermelon, 120
German carob torte, 61

Gift-wrapped apples with vanilla sauce, 22
Ginger, 5
  apple, pudding, New Year's, 62
  cutout, cookies, 50
  gingerbread characters, 47
Gingerbread characters, 47
Ginger root, spiced wine, 45
Glazed blueberry pie, 119
Glazed oranges, 146–47
Glazed peach pie, 119
Glazed walnuts, 80
Glorified pineapple rice, 90
Gluten flour, 8, 9, 12
Gluten flour bread mix, 12
Grapefruit, broiled, 98
Grape juice:
  purple, patriotic soda, 140
  white, 11
    grape mousse, 117
    spiced wine, 45
Grapes, grape mousse, 117

Hain strawberry concentrate, 10
Halloween foods, 141–60
  apple(s):
    butter custard, 153
    caramel, 158
    carob coconut candied, 160
    peanut butter caramel, 159
  banana and sweet potato casserole, 144
  carrot:
    cookies, 155
    pudding, 147
  children's trick-o'-treats, 158–60
    caramel apples, 158

Halloween foods (*cont.*)
    carob coconut candied apples, 160
    corn and peanut "jacks," 159
    peanut butter caramel apples, 159
    peanut butter popcorn balls, 158
  compote, 144–45
  orange:
    balls, 154
    Bavarian, 143–44
    cake, open face, 151–52
    cheesecake, 152
    -cranberry torte, 148–49
    cream puffs, 156–57
    glazed, 146–47
    haystacks, 156
    meringue, 142
    meringue pie, 147–48
  popcorn:
    balls, peanut butter, 158
    fudge, 154
  pumpkin:
    cake, 149–50
    cookies, 155–56
    parfait, 146
    soufflé, 145
    sweet stuffed, 143
    tarts, 157
  sweet potato:
    and banana casserole, 144
    cake with raisin sauce, 150–51
  yam pudding, 153
Hanukkah treats. *See* Christmas-Hanukkah treats
Heart-shaped caramel pops, 85
Honey, 4, 5
  calories in, 6

Honeydew. *See* Melon(s)
Hot apple cranberry punch, 181
Hot cross buns, 107
How to Get Well (Airola), 7
Hypoglycemics, 7

Indian pudding, 166
Italian meringues, 75

Jelled hearts, 84
Jelled sherried fruit, 116
Jelly:
  coffee, 97
  roll, old-fashioned, 99
Joe Froggers, 38–39

Latkes, dessert, 33
Layered peanut butter carob toffee, 76
Lechithin, granular, 13
Lemon:
  almond sandwich crème cookies, 39–40
  doughnuts, 101
  loaf, 102
  sauce, molasses marble cake with, 89–90
Lemon peel, 5
Lollipops, heart-shaped caramel, 85
Low blood sugar. *See* Hypoglycemics
Low calorie eggless crêpes, 18

Macaroon balls, sherried, 37
Malt, 5
  liquid barley, 11
Maple syrup, 4, 5
Marble cake, molasses, with lemon sauce, 89–90

Melon(s):
    pastel parfaits, 117–18
    sherbet-stuffed, 115
    summer eggnog, 134
    unsweetened frozen, balls, 10
        pastel punch, 112
    watermelon gelatin, 120
Meringue(s):
    café au lait, 109
    Italian, 75
    mushrooms, 106
    orange(s), 142
        pie, 147–48
Milk:
    apple butter custard, 153
    calories in, 6
    carob coconut candied apples, 160
    carrot pudding, 147
    cold carob, 135
    cold mocha, 135
    éclairs, 99–100
    eggnog:
        strawberry, 83
        summer, 134
    floating islands, 29
    fresh fruit and custard roll, 129
    meringue:
        café au lait, 109
        oranges, 142
    orange cream puffs, 156–57
    pumpkin:
        parfait, 146
        sweet stuffed, 143
    raisin turmeric, 182
    raspberry cream pie, 126–27
    red, white and blue pie, 136–37

    strawberry:
        eggnog, 83
        hot, 86
    yam pudding, 153
Milk powder, non-instant skim, 5, 6, 13
    buttery snowballs, 63
    milk ball angels, 50
    mocha balls, 83
    popcorn fudge, 154
"Mincemeat" pie, 168
Mineral water:
    patriotic soda, 140
    sparkling pink punch, 136
Mint and carob:
    layered dessert, 95–96
    log, 81
    sandwich cookies, 40
Mocha:
    balls, 83
    cold, 135
    fancy, 109
Molasses:
    blackstrap. *See* Blackstrap molasses
    marble cake with lemon sauce, 89–90
    table, 4, 11
Mousse:
    applesauce, 56
    carob, 73
    grape, 117
    pastel parfaits, 117–18
    raisin nut, 28
    sherry apple, 56–57
Mulled cider, 46
Mushrooms, meringue, 106

New Year's treats, 51–63
  almond tarts, Swedish, 58
  apple(s):
    applesauce mousse, 56
    ginger pudding, 62
    prune strudel, 60
    sherry, mousse, 56–57
    snow, 52
    turnovers with cardamom sauce,
      59
    walnut cheesecake, creamy, 57
  bananas:
    baked, with almond sauce,
      fancy, 55
    cranberry, cream delight,
      55–56
  buttery snowballs, 63
  carob:
    cheesecake, 58–59
    peanut waffles, 62–63
    torte, German, 61
  cheesecake:
    carob, 58–59
    creamy apple walnut, 57
  cranberry banana cream delight,
    55–56
  fruit:
    compote in wine sauce, winter,
      54
    soup, Swedish, 53
  pears:
    cheese-stuffed, 53
    whole scarlet, 53–54
  sesame rice ring, 60
  sherry apple mousse, 56–57
Nut(s):
  bonbons, cream cheese, 82
  -coated caramels, 77

  English toffee, 82
  -filled horns, 105
  raisin, mousse, 28
  see also specific types of nuts
Nutmeg, 5

Old-fashioned jelly roll, 99
Open face orange cake, 151–52
Orange(s):
  baked, soufflé, 93
  balls, Halloween, 154
  Bavarian, 96, 143–44
  cake:
    cheesecake, 152
    open face, 151–52
  cinnamon:
    drink, hot, 182
    rolls, 103–104
  cookies, delicate, 42
  cranberry:
    mold, 163–64
    torte, 148–49
  cream puffs, 156–57
  glazed, 146–47
  haystacks, 156
  meringue, 142
  pie, 147–48
  pumpkin, currant pie, 170–
    71
  sauce, baked pears in, 167
Orange peel, 5

Pancakes, yogurt cheese, Hanukkah,
  32
Parfaits:
  pastel, 117–18
  pineapple, 97
  pumpkin, 146

Parfaits (*cont.*)
strawberry:
carob, 74
ice cream, 116
tahini, walnut, coffee, 166–67
tapioca plum, 30–31
Pastel punch, 112
Pastry dough:
cream puff, 9, 19
flaky, 16
stretchy, 16
Patriotic soda, 140
Peach(es):
coconut cupcakes, 131
and cream cake, 121
fresh baked, 122–23
pie, glazed, 119
soufflé, fresh, 120–21
strudel, 127
summer eggnog, 134
trifle, 88
unsweetened canned, 10
unsweetened frozen, 10
Peanut butter:
caramel apples, 159
carob:
toffee, layered, 76
wafers, 62–63
popcorn balls, 158
Peanuts and corn "jacks," 159
Pears:
cheese-stuffed, 53
in orange sauce, baked, 167
unsweetened canned, 10
whole scarlet, 53–54
Pecan(s):
clusters, caramel, 80
cream cheese nut bonbons, 82
pralines, 81

Peppermint extract, 5
Peppermint tea:
carob mint:
layered dessert, 95–96
sandwich cookies, 40
Pero, 11
Persimmon sherbet, 114
Pie(s):
apple:
chestnut, 169
cranberry nut, 169
mince crumb, 30
"mincemeat," 168
blueberry, glazed, 119
chestnut apple, 169
chiffon:
carob, 72
pineapple, 97
strawberry, 72–73, 118
cranberry:
apple, nut, 169
Christmas, 28
"mincemeat," 168
orange:
meringue, 147–48
pumpkin, currant, 170–71
peach, glazed, 119
piña colada meringue, 95
plum, with chestnut sauce, 25–26
pumpkin:
classic, 167–68
orange, currant, 170–71
raspberry cream, 126–27
red, white and blue, 136–37
strawberry:
chiffon, 72–73, 118
ricotta, 126
yam applesauce, 165

Pie crusts, techniques for whole
  grain, 9
Piña colada:
  meringue pie, 95
  punch, 136
Pineapple:
  bread, 103
  chiffon pie, 97
  parfaits, 98
  piña colada punch, 136
  rice, glorified, 90
  sauce, simple avocado sherbet
    with, 115
  soufflé, 92
  tea rings, 108
  unsweetened canned, 10
Pineapple juice, 10
  concentrate, 10
  pastel punch, 112
  piña colada punch, 136
Pinwheels, 38
Plum(s):
  apple cobbler, 26
  parfaits, tapioca, 30–31
  in pastry, 132
  pie with chestnut sauce, 25–26
  pudding, English, 44–45
  stuffed, 35
Popcorn:
  bunny, big, 110
  corn and peanut "jacks," 159
  fudge, 154
Popsicles, striped, 140
Potatoes:
  dessert latkes, 33
  sweet:
    balls, 170
    and banana casserole, 144

cake with raisin sauce, 150–51
  yam pudding, 153
Pralines, 81
Prevention magazine, 7
Profiteroles, strawberry, with carob
    sauce, 67–68
Protein, 7, 9
Prune(s):
  apple strudel, 60
  Bundt cake, 175
  stuffed plums, 35
  tapioca plum parfaits, 30–31
Pudding:
  apple ginger, New Year's, 62
  banana, with cranberry sauce,
    steamed, 34–35
  carrot, 147
  Christmas apple cheese bread, 25
  English plum, 44–45
  Indian, 166
  yam, 153
Pumpkin:
  bread, 172
  cake, 149–50
  cookies, 155–56
  flan, caramel, 162
  Halloween compote, 144–45
  parfait, 146
  pie:
    classic, 167–68
    orange, currant, 170–71
  soufflé, 145
  sweet stuffed, 143
  tarts, 157
Punch:
  apple cranberry, hot, 181
  pastel, 112
  piña colada, 136

Punch (*cont.*)
  Rosie, 84
  sparkling pink, 136

Raisin(s):
  chestnut strudel, 179
  English plum pudding, 44–45
  Halloween compote, 144–45
  "mincemeat" pie, 168
  nut mousse, 28
  sauce, sweet potato cake with, 150–51
  sesame clusters, 79
  sweet stuffed pumpkins, 143
  turmeric milk, 182
Raspberry(ies):
  cream pie, 126–27
  strudel, 127
  zabaglione, 124
Red, white and blue gelatin, 139
Red, white and blue pie, 136–37
Red Zinger tea, sparkling pink punch, 136
Refrigerator carob cheesecake, 71
Repeatedly used recipes, 15–19
Rice:
  apple fritters with sesame sauce, 164
  pineapple, glorified, 90
  sesame, ring, 60
  sweet stuffed pumpkin, 143
Ricotta cheese, skim milk, 6
  blintzes, Eastern breakfast, 91
  carob strawberry cheese roll, 69–70
  cheesecake:
    carob, 58–59
    orange, 152

cranberry cheese mold, 171–72
mint carob layered dessert, 95–96
orange:
  Bavarian, 96
  -cranberry torte, 148–49
pineapple:
  parfaits, 98
  rice, glorified, 90
red, white and blue gelatin, 139
sherry apple mousse, 56–57
strawberry:
  cream gelatin, 120
  crêpes, 75–76
  profiteroles with carob sauce, 67–68
  ricotta pie, 126
  Romanoff, 123
  shortcake, 122
  -stuffed pear, 53
Rolls, orange cinnamon, 103–104
Rosie punch, 84
Rumford's baking powder, 13

Safflower oil, 12
Sauce:
  almond, fancy baked bananas with, 55
  applesauce:
    Bundt cake, 177–78
    cranberry, baked cranberry apple dumplings with, 162–63
    mousse, 56
    pie, yam, 165
  cardamom, apple turnovers with, 59
  carob:
    easy banana sherbet with hot, 114

Sauce (*cont.*)
 strawberry profiteroles with, 67–68
 chestnut, plum pie with, 25–26
 coffee walnut, 166–67
 cranberry, steamed banana pudding with, 34–35
 lemon, molasses marble cake with, 89–90
 orange, baked pears in, 167
 pineapple, avocado sherbet with, simple, 115
 plum, tapioca plum parfaits, 30–31
 raisin, sweet potato cake with, 150–51
 sesame, apple fritters with, 164
 vanilla, gift-wrapped apples with, 22
 wine, winter fruit compote in, 54
Sesame seeds, raisin, clusters, 79
Sesame tahini, 13
 apple fritters with sesame sauce, 164
 rice ring, 60
 walnut, coffee parfaits, 166–67
Sherbet:
 avocado, with pineapple sauce, simple, 115
 banana, with hot carob sauce, easy, 114
 persimmon, 114
 -stuffed melons, 115
Sherry(ied):
 apple mousse, 56–57
 fruit, jelled, 116
 macaroon balls, 37
Snow apples, 52
Soda, patriotic, 140

Soufflé(s):
 apple, individual, 29
 apricot, baked, 94
 crème de menthe, 93–94
 orange baked, 93
 peach, fresh, 120–21
 pineapple, 92
 pumpkin, 145
Soup, Swedish fruit, 53
Soy flour, 8, 9, 12
Sparkling pink punch, 136
Spiced wine, 45
Strawberry(ies):
 cake, 124–25
  flag, 138–39
  shortcake, 122
 carob:
  cheese roll, 69–70
  frozen, 85
  parfaits, 74
 chiffon pie, 72–73, 118
 concentrate, 10
 crêpes, 75–76
 egg nog, 83
  summer, 134
 flag cake, 138–39
 hot milk, 86
 ice cream parfaits, 116
 Italian meringues, 75
 patriotic soda, 140
 profiteroles with carob sauce, 67–68
 punch:
  Rosie, 84
  sparkling pink, 136
 red, white and blue gelatin, 139
 red, white and blue pie, 136–37
 ricotta pie, 126

Strawberry(ies) (*cont.*)
shortcake, 122
striped popsicles, 140
strudel, 127
tarts:
glazed, 132–33
Valentine's, 74
turnovers, 125
unsweetened frozen, 10
whole scarlet pears, 54–55
zabaglione, 124
Strawberry-apple juice, sparkling
pink punch, 136
Strawberry juice, jelled hearts,
84
Stretchy pastry dough, 16
Striped popsicles, 140
Strudel, 17–18
apple prune, 60
raisin chestnut, 179
strawberry, 127
techniques for whole wheat, 9
Strufoli, 66
Stuffed dates, 35
Stuffed plums, 35
Sugar, 4, 5, 6, 8
calories in, 6
Summer eggnog, 134
Sunflower oil, 12
Swedish almond tarts, 58
Swedish fruit soup, 53
Swedish glogg, 46
Swedish tea ring, 43–44
Sweet croissants, 180–81
Sweet dough figures, 48
Sweet potato:
balls, 170
and banana casserole, 144

cake with raisin sauce, 150–51
see also Yam(s)
Sweet stuffed pumpkin, 143

Tahini. *See* Sesame tahini
Tapioca plum parfaits, 30–31
Tarts:
almond, Swedish, 58
baby walnut date, 37
pumpkin, 157
strawberry:
glazed, 132–33
Valentine's, 74
Tea ring:
pineapple, 108
Swedish, 43–44
Thanksgiving desserts, 161–82
apple:
applesauce Bundt cake, 177–78
applesauce pie, yam, 165
cranberry punch, hot, 181
dumplings, baked cranberry,
with cranberry applesauce,
162–63
-filled doughnuts, 179–80
fritters with sesame sauce, 164
pie, chestnut, 169
pie, cranberry nut, 169
rings, French fried, 165
carrot cake, 176–77
chestnut:
knots, 178
pie, apple, 169
strudel, raisin, 179
cranberry:
apple punch, hot, 181
baked, apple dumplings, with
cranberry applesauce, 162–63

Thanksgiving desserts (*cont.*)
    bread, 173
    cheese mold, 171–72
    coffee ring, 173–74
    nut pie, apple, 169
    orange, mold, 163–64
  croissants, sweet, 180–81
  Indian pudding, 166
  "mincemeat" pie, 168
  orange:
    cinnamon drink, hot, 182
    cranberry mold, 163–64
    pumpkin, currant pie, 170–71
    sauce, baked pears in, 167
  pears in orange sauce, baked, 167
  pumpkin:
    bread, 172
    flan, caramel, 162
    orange, currant pie, 170–71
    pie, classic, 167–68
  raisin:
    chestnut strudel, 179
    turmeric milk, 182
  sweet potato balls, 170
  tahini:
    apple fritters with sesame sauce,
      164
    walnut, coffee parfaits, 166–67
  zucchini bread, 175–76
Toffee:
  English, 82
  layered peanut butter carob, 76
Torte:
  carob, German, 61
  cranberry-orange, 148–49
Trifle:
  English Christmas, 31–32
  peach, 88
Turmeric milk, raisin, 182

Turnovers:
  apple, with cardamom sauce, 59
  strawberry, 125

Valentine's Day treats, 65–86
  almond crunch, 77
  Black Forest cake, 68–69
  caramel(s):
    cream, 79
    nut-coated, 77
    pecan clusters, 80
    pops, heart-shaped, 85
  carob:
    cake, 70–71
    capped coconut chews, 78
    cheesecake, refrigerator, 71
    chiffon pie, 72
    fondue, 67
    frozen, strawberries, 85
    log, mint, 81
    mousse, 73
    sauce, strawberry profiteroles
      with, 67–68
    strawberry, parfaits, 74
    strawberry cheese roll, 69–70
    toffee, layered peanut butter, 76
  for children, 84–86
    frozen carob strawberries, 85
    heart-shaped caramel pops, 85
    jelled hearts, 84
    strawberry hot milk, 86
  coconut chews:
    carob capped, 78
    molasses, 78
  Italian meringues, 75
  mocha balls, 83
  nut(s):
    bonbons, cream cheese, 82

Valentine's Day treats (*cont.*)
    -coated caramels, 77
    English toffee, 82
  pecans:
    caramel, clusters, 80
    praline, 81
  raisin sesame clusters, 79
  strawberry(ies):
    carob, cheese roll, 69–70
    carob, frozen, 85
    carob parfaits, 74
    chiffon pie, 72–73
    crêpes, 75–76
    eggnog, 83
    hot milk, 86
    jelled hearts, 84
    profiteroles with carob sauce, 67–68
    Rosie punch, 84
    tarts, 74
  strufoli, 66
  walnuts, glazed, 80
Vanilla extract, 5
Vanilla sauce, gift-wrapped apples with, 22

Wafers, carob peanut, 62–63
Walnut(s):
  cheesecake, creamy apple, 57
  cream cheese nut bonbons, 82
  date tarts, baby, 37
  glazed, 80
  "mincemeat" pie, 168
  nut-filled horns, 105–106
  raisin nut mousse, 28
  tahini, coffee parfaits, 166–67

Watermelon gelatin, 120
Welch's grape juice, 11
Whipped cream, 6
Whole grains, 4, 7
  unique techniques for light desserts from, 8–10
  see also specific whole grain flours,
    e.g. Gluten flour; Soy flour
Whole scarlet pears, 53–54
Whole wheat pastry flour, 8–9, 12
  cream puff pastry, 19
  crêpes:
    delicate whole wheat, 18
    low calorie eggless, 18
  crumble crust, 17
  pastry dough:
    flaky, 16
    stretchy, 16
  strudel, 17–18
Wine:
  sauce, winter fruit compote in, 54
  spiced, 45
  Swedish glogg, 46
Winter fruit compote in wine sauce, 54

Yam(s), 7
  applesauce pie, 165
  pudding, 153
  see also Sweet potato
Yogurt cheese pancakes, Hanukkah, 32

Zucchini bread, 175–76

DATE DUE

DEC 16 '83			